ANCIENT CHINA

TO THE GREAT WALL...AND BEYOND

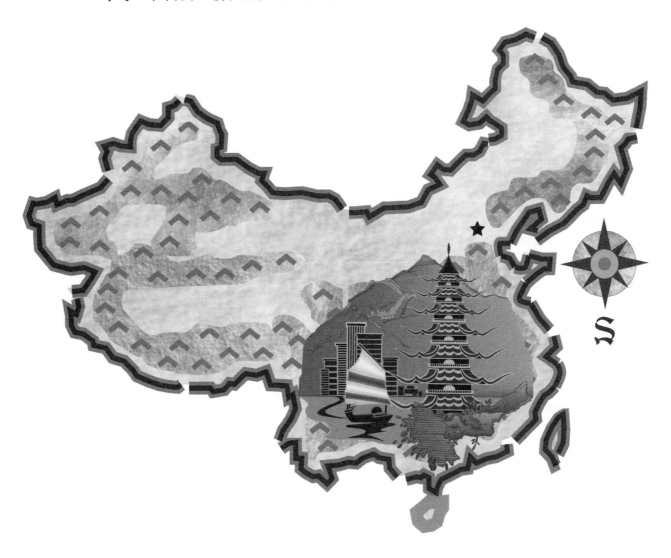

Zeezok
publishing

Elyria, OH

Ancient China:

To the Great Wall...and Beyond

by Judy Wilcox

ISBN-10: 0-9746505-0-1
ISBN-13: 978-0-9746505-0-0

Copyright 2003

Published by:
Zeezok Publishing
PO Box 1960
Elyria OH 44036

www.Zeezok.com
1-800-749-1681

This book is lovingly dedicated to my parents,

Daniel and Mary Gehman,

who have given me a love of reading and learning. The example you have been for me as students of God's Word is an example I hope to emulate as consistently for my children.

Acknowledgments

This writing project would never have been accomplished, let alone *started*, without the help and exhortation of a number of individuals. I need to thank the following:

Maggie Hogan, for giving me the notion that I should try writing a chapter, which eventually turned into this book. I'm going to be wary about any more "inspirations" you get in the early morning hours, though!

Tyler Hogan, for providing the maps for the book. It is exciting to see how God is using your talents and gifts to His glory—and how you are *allowing* Him to do so.

Kathryn Dix and Kirsten Spickler, for diligently and patiently proofreading, editing, and improving this first attempt at authorship.

Diana Waring, Rebecca Berg, and Steve & Jane Lambert, for their suggestions and tips on how to make this book more user-friendly.

Heather Duffy, Rebecca Simmons, and Sharon Thomas, for answering the phones and managing the office at different times during this long writing venture. Your efforts helped me maintain what little sanity I have left so I could write.

Jack and Carol Wilcox, for taking the children for the afternoon at various points in the writing process. Those quiet moments were inexpressibly helpful for me, plus they were moments of creating special memories with your grandchildren. The entire family thanks you for those memories. I am truly blessed to have such godly, loving in-laws.

Dan and Mary Gehman, for giving me time at the beginning of this project to formulate an overall outline and major notes—all by just coming to Ohio for a three-week visit and spoiling the family sweetly. Imagine what I could accomplish if you left Big Sky Country for the Buckeye State. I love you!

The Charlie & Renee Olson family, the Kurt & Faye Wilcox family, and the Jeff & Kathy Wilcox family, for your interest in and prayers for our family during this project. How thankful I am for a sister, sisters-in-law, and brothers-in-law (with their families) who are living testimonies of God's grace and goodness.

Derek, Westley, Bethany, and Jennifer—my four beloved children—for your patience, enthusiasm, and encouragement throughout the past two years. Not only did you give me time to write, but you were also willing participants in our first attempts at using this unit study. I love you and I pray that you will always be interested in sharing the Gospel with a world in need.

Kris, my heartening and supportive husband, for doing the layout of the book, washing dishes, scrubbing kids, reminding me of our goal, and believing that this book could become a reality. "I love you" seems so inadequate, yet what else can I say to express how deeply blessed I am to have you in my life as my spiritual leader, lover, and best friend?

God our Father and the Lord Jesus Christ, for continually impressing upon me throughout this study that it is by grace I have been saved through faith, and that not of myself; it is the gift of God, not of works, lest I should boast (Eph. 2:8, 9). I am humbled to be a part of Your family. May You be honored by and pleased with this work, for there is no point in writing or laboring otherwise.

Table of Contents

Avoiding the "Drone Zone"

It was another stuffy day in world history class. Perhaps you can recall a similar incident in *your* education. The 50-minute period began with you propping your textbook open on the desk, taking out a folder of paper, poising your pen for note taking, and then listening intently as the teacher read directly from the textbook. Well, in my experience, I listened intently for all of five seconds, and then I began writing notes furiously. No, I was not writing notes on the historical data being droned through my ears. I was writing notes to classmates who were equally glassy-eyed and bored.

That was my junior year of high school history, and while I remember nothing of what I memorized for each test in that class, that class changed my life. It caused me to promise that I would never teach in the "drone zone." So far, it is a vow I have been able to uphold, both in teaching at a local school and in teaching my children at home. Oh, there were times when I needed to use the lecture approach—when presenting certain concepts or when working with certain groups of students. There have even been times that I have needed to read portions of a textbook directly to my students (including my own children) to relay information correctly. Yet, I have never desired to convey material or educate in the lecture mode on a consistent basis.

History is too exciting to relegate to textbooks, short answer questions, and tests. It is not dull or dead (unless we make it that way or kill it). History is units of time in various cultures; it is events and circumstances that happened to real people like you and me; it is life on a continuum. History is heart, soul, mind, and experience, not merely dates, vocabulary words, and an occasional paragraph-long biography.

And history is much more enjoyable and so much more memorable when it is studied in a lively manner, which is what unit studies enable homeschooling families to encounter. History unit studies afford an incredible opportunity to show our children how God is in control of everything. From the first cloud in nature to the last pharaoh in Egypt, from the point at which Adam named the animals to the naming of the U.S. president in the last election, from the moment time began to the present moment, God knows and cares about what is happening! Unit studies allow families to delve into those moments and to appreciate God's sovereignty and grace all the more thoroughly.

Chapter 1
What Is a "Unit Study"?

By way of quick definition, "unit study" means that you incorporate as many different subjects as possible into one area of study. A historical period, historical event, or key person can serve as the springboard for your unit, and from that main theme branch other topics of study beyond history—including geography (physical and cultural), language arts, science, the fine arts, home management, and more. Unit studies also may be centered on a specific character quality, scientific discovery, work of literature, health topic, and so forth. The main focus of the unit study in *Ancient China: To the Great Wall...and Beyond* will be on the history of China, its major dynasties in particular.

A variety of ages can be taught at the same time using the unit study approach because age-appropriate books can be provided for each grade of student, while the key information or outline of material remains the same for all ages. Unit studies also allow you to employ many different media and resources (books, foods, paintings, videos, models, even plastic construction blocks) in the study. Just a side note: Some people include math as part of their unit studies, but I believe my children need a more traditional, systematic course for math concepts. So asking them to determine catapult trajectory ranges or add up the yards of material used in clipper ship sails typically does not count as our math for the day.

My intent in any unit study is to introduce the children to as many key people, places, events, and concepts as possible. I'm giving them "hooks," basically. Picture a long row of coat hooks in your child's mind. Each hook has a label near it indicating that it is the hook for Simon Kenton, the Boer War, electric eels, and so forth. As the child first encounters each new topic in his studies, he places a hook and a backpack for further data on the hook. With each new bit of information he receives, the child deposits a "book" in the appropriate backpack on the corresponding hook.

Sometimes our unit study will touch on only certain characters or events, while other elements of the unit study will be presented in much more in detail and depth. With K–6 students, I assume that they are going to encounter these people and concepts again at some point in their studies, so I'm not too stressed about making sure they know everything they can about Virginia Dare or the Peloponnesian War. But they should be familiar enough with the information that the next time they hear those words, their ears prick up and lightbulbs glow as they collect new information to add to their "hooks." Time is limited in our studies—at least the time that I can direct their learning specifically. Yet, I want my children to be stretched mentally, to research their natural questions when they arise, and to discover exciting facts on their own. In essence, I want them to know that thinking and education take effort, but the rewards of knowledge and growth are worth that effort.

Two activities that we maintain throughout a history unit are a timeline and student copybooks. We add figures to our world timeline on the wall, or we make smaller timelines (with figures for events from around the world) for the particular period of history we're studying. It makes the jigsaw puzzle of world history fit together a bit more logically. We recently tried creating a homemade timeline book because our wall timeline was becoming too convoluted. We like the convenience of having the figures in a large book/portfolio to which we can add more figures later, but I miss having the timeline out and visible where it is easily referenced. You'll have to decide which format will work best for your family. (We *highly* recommend Amy Pak's *History Through the Ages Historical Timeline Figures* for use with any style of timeline—wall, book, portfolio, pre-published, etc. See the bibliography for more details on her timeline packets.)

The second activity we maintain throughout a unit study is individual student copybooks. Student copybooks are sentences or paragraphs of information about our daily studies in the unit. Older students can take notes in their copybooks as we're reading from the various resources or take notes after we've completed our work for the day. Younger students can dictate or copy from resources (or their dictation) the information they would like to include in their copybooks about the day's topic. In either case, a copybook contains the information each child considers most important and memorable. This personalized copybook is also where any art projects or illustrations related to the unit will be compiled. By the end of each unit, then, they have a book of material on the subject, and they are creating their own "Books of Knowledge" library for later reference.

The final key element of any unit study is to read, and read, and read about your unit. Read *with* your children as much as possible. Enjoy your discoveries and new learning experiences as a family! Since you are not Supermom or Superdad, however, the reality is that sometimes your older students will need to read pages, chapters, or even entire books on their own. Use those self-directed readings as springboards for discussion at the supper table, or have your older students teach what they learned in their independent reading to their younger siblings. Remember, you're trying to place lots of hooks on the walls of your children's minds, hooks on which to hang more information about a wide variety of subjects and concepts. Not all those hooks have to be nailed in by mom or dad, nor do all the "books" in the imaginary backpacks on those hooks have to be read *aloud* to each child by a parent.

Chapter 2
Why Go Beyond the Great Wall?

Silkworms, rice paddies, Mongolian warriors, nightingales, pagodas, and the Great Wall—all are images conjured by the word China. Yes, China (also known as Cathay in ancient times) is a country whose history extends far beyond Marco Polo's travels and a few recognizable dynasty names. It actually had an established dynasty along the Yangtze River some 200 years before the Egyptian pharaohs came into power along the Nile River. China is a land of diverse climates, geographical landforms, and ethnic groups. As you explore this country's remarkable history, the more you recognize the impact it has made scientifically, religiously, historically, and artistically throughout the world. The richness and uniqueness of China's culture and history should be a part of any homeschooler's education.

Ancient China: To the Great Wall…and Beyond devotes approximately two weeks on geography (physical and cultural), several weeks on 11 major dynasties in China's history, and at least part of a week on how dynasties have given way to Communism in modern China. Usually for our family, we have discovered that six-week or eight-week units seem to work best, but for more extensive topics a 12-week session may be necessary. The more research I did on China, the more I realized a 12-week study would be required to do China any justice.

In the following lessons, we have provided questions and projects to pursue for the unit on China, and we've supplied answers or informative text to complete the process. You can read portions of this text with your children, but we would highly advise getting supplemental books (from the bibliography, or from your own research) to go along with the subtopics so that your elementary students begin to appreciate the informative resources available at the library. For your convenience in using the annotated bibliography, the author's name as well as the title of the book are given when a source is cited.

If you are unable to find precisely the same books that are suggested in the text of this unit study or in the bibliography, don't panic. Try using interlibrary loan to obtain the titles that are not in your local library, and then use the resources that *are* in your library. You will find plenty of books in your library's stacks that are more than adequate to replace any missing titles from our suggested list.

Please look over the lesson plans for the next week in advance so that you can get any additional book resources, project items, videos, and so forth beforehand. This advance reading also prepares you for what subtopics you will be learning about with each dynasty.

Recommended items to have ready are listed at the beginning of each dynasty. We further encourage you to do a wide range of these activities, rounding out your unit all the more fully. We have used symbols for each type of activity to help you incorporate a variety of subjects within this history unit.

Project Symbols

⧗	History
❀	Geography (physical and cultural)
✏	Language Arts (writing, poetry, etc.)
📖	Reading Selections
♪	Fine Arts – Music (CDs, cassettes, live concerts, etc.)
🖌	Fine Arts - Art
✂	Hands-On Activities (crafts, models, recipes, etc.)
🚀	Science
📺	Audio/Visual Resources (DVDs, videocassettes, etc.)
⚲	Research Skills
💡	Critical Thinking
🚐	Field Trip Ideas

We have tried to supply daily lesson suggestions. They are exactly that: *suggestions*. Realize that you can pace these lessons to suit your family's needs. If you want to spend longer on certain dynasties or projects, do it! If you don't want to spend as long on a certain portion of the study, choose to do only one of the activities or lesson ideas for each day, or combine suggested activities even more. The beauty of homeschooling lessons is that they can be tailored to *your* family's interests, needs, and wants…so tailor them without hesitation.

Now, to the Great Wall…and beyond!

Chapter 3
Geography Lessons for China

Recommended Items

- ❑ Map of world or globe
- ❑ Reproducible maps of China in Appendix C for labeling sites
- ❑ Stamp collection or Chinese art books
- ❑ Reference books on unusual animals in the Far East
- ❑ Large pan and lid
- ❑ Sandbox or ditch for construction of a dam
- ❑ Origami books
- ❑ Tea
- ❑ Rice cakes
- ❑ Kite
- ❑ Tangram, Chinese checkers, pick-up sticks, mah-jongg, or other Chinese games
- ❑ Travel video of China

Day 1

❁ Find China on a map or globe. What is the size of the country of China (land mass and current population)?

> China is considered part of the "Far East" on the continent of Asia. It is the third largest nation in the world, after Russia and Canada, and is composed of 3,685,000 square miles. But it has the largest population in the world (1,237,000,000 people). Almost one out of every five humans on the planet lives in China. What a mission field!

❁ From where you live, what would be the fastest route to fly to China? From east to west, or vice versa?

> Use a piece of yarn to measure the difference in distance.

❁ Map major mountain ranges, deserts, bodies of water, rivers, cities, man-made rarities, and surrounding seas and countries. Let the student determine his own symbols for these various elements and maintain a map key for his individual map. Younger students may need help *labeling* these different sites, but they should be attempting to draw the basic route or location of each of these features on their own, making it a personal project. I used Wynn Kapit's *The Geography Coloring Book* to help accumulate the majority of this information. We have supplied reproducible maps of China and the surrounding geography in the back of the book, for your convenience. (Rivers and bodies of water are indicated but not labeled.)

> Include the Yangtze, Pearl, and Yellow rivers; the Grand Canal; the Great Wall of China; the territories of Hong Kong, Macao, and Taiwan; the Gobi desert; the Turpan Depression; the Himalayas (over 30 peaks standing higher than 28,200 feet!); major cities like Beijing (Peking), Canton (Guangzhou), and Shanghai; the Yellow, East China, and South China seas; and Hainan Island. Also indicate where the equator and Tropic of Cancer lines run through the country. These lines help put the climate into perspective later on.

Day 2

❋ Currently, what are the five autonomous regions in China? Indicate these regions on the map. Again, *The Geography Coloring Book* or *Everyday Geography* (by Kevin McKinney) helps provide these facts.

> Tibet—southwestern borders; Manchuria—northeast, the major industrial and agricultural region; Inner Mongolia—north central uplands (including part of the Gobi desert), but different from Mongolia, the country; Xinjiang—northwest (including the Tian Shan mountains, Taklimakan desert, and Turpan Depression); and China Proper—eastern lowlands, central and southeastern uplands. To read more about these regions, consider *The Provinces and Cities of China*, by Lynn Stone.

✂ Use a stamp collection or browse through books containing art from China to determine what elements of life are of cultural significance to the Chinese.

> Flowers, birds, jade, natural scenes, and fine pottery are consistent themes.

🚀 What animals and plants are unique or special to the region? Your average encyclopedia or an illustrated animal book like *The Kingfisher Illustrated Animal Encyclopedia* will provide a good basis for this portion of research. Make a poster of pictures that show these elements of nature. You could also have your student write short captions of information about each item on the poster. Display the poster for the remainder of the unit.

Pekingese dog

🗝 You could study: Siberian tigers, tapirs, pandas, lesser (or red) pandas, Asiatic black bears, sun bears, snow leopards, Asian elephants, orangutans, yaks, pugs, Pekingese dogs, Mandarin ducks, golden pheasants, common goldcrests, cormorants, nightingales, gray herons, crickets, praying mantises, forest musk deer, chevrotain, Chinese muntjacs, bamboo, rice, peonies, lotus blossoms, millet, hemp, ginseng, ginger, and tea. (This portion of study inevitably reminds us of God's creativity and love of beauty.)

📖 Two books by Demi, *Kites* and *Happy New Year! Kung-Hsi Fa-Ts'ai!,* reveal the symbolism or association made with various plants and animals praised by the Chinese. Be aware, however, that these books do not judge Chinese mysticism in any manner.

Day 3

❋ What is the climate of the area? *The Geography Coloring Book* provides some information on the general temperatures of the regions, but *Everyday Geography* better explains monsoons. You can use a standard almanac or perhaps a resource like *FACTS Plus* (by Susan Anthony) to gain more data, as well.

💡 Most of China's climate is humid and subtropical. Summers in the majority of the regions are hot, while in Tibet they are mild. Why would Tibet's summers be mild? Consider the influence of the Himalayas on weather and temperatures! Rainfall averages vary from region to region. In the north, 20 to 40 inches of rain a year is typical. In the west and central regions, 40 to 60 inches annually is common. And along the east coast and the Tropic of Cancer, 60 to 80 inches of rain is expected each year. Much of this rain along the coast is the result of monsoons. (Words in bold font within the text are words that appear in the glossary and could be used as vocabulary cards for review.) **Monsoon** actually comes from the Arabic word *mawsim*, which means "season." It refers to the periodic wind system that causes the wet and dry weather in India and southern Asia. Summer monsoons predominantly involve winds and heavy rain. When the trade winds from the northeast and southeast collide around the equator, air rises, atmospheric pressure falls, and condensation forms clouds that produce heavy precipitation. Another way to picture it is that in the summer, heat over Asia creates low pressure over most of the continent, while warm, moist air is drawn up from the Indian Ocean, which results in rain-producing clouds. In the autumn there is less of a contrast between the land and sea temperatures, so the areas of low and high pressure reverse. The result is cooler, drier air blowing down from the Himalayas, which persists until spring.

- ⚲ How do the climate and geographical features influence China's food, transportation, farming, and industry?

    Monsoons often result in tremendous crop loss and famine, because of both too much rain or not enough rain at the right time. The rainy season in China varies, but usually it occurs from April to October. If lots of warm, moist air over the Indian Ocean collides with the heated land mass, heavy rains are likely—causing floods and ruining crops. If monsoons arrive late, less rain falls, and crops are lost. Remember the population of China. What do you think happens when crops are poor in such a populous nation? Right, *famine* occurs.

- 🚀 Create a miniature monsoon. **(Adult supervision, please!)** Boil water in a pan. Add ice cubes to the boiling water and observe how the mixing of different temperatures affects the surrounding environment. Now place the lid on the pan for a short period of time; lift to observe how rapidly moisture forms on the lid. This moisture is basically cloud formation, as one would experience on a large scale in a monsoon.

- ✎ Older students could write a short research paper on monsoons—including their formation, locations, effects on land and mankind, and so forth.

Day 4

- ⚲ How is river life in China important in farming, fishing, and transporting goods?

    The Yellow and Yangtze rivers are key to China's farming and industry. Both are major avenues for transporting goods and crops from interior China to the coast. In fact, the Yangtze River flows through China's commercial region and ends at one of the world's busiest ports, Shanghai. (Make sure Shanghai is labeled on your maps from Day 1.)

Use Three Gorges Dam timeline figure in Appendix C

📖 Read *The Story About Ping*, by Marjorie Flack and Kurt Wiese, to gain a sense of life on the Yangtze River. Also notice the unique method of fishing, using **cormorants** with bands around their necks (preventing them from swallowing the fish they bring to the surface) when reading Flack's classic young reader.

A controversial project currently underway on the Yangtze River is the Three Gorges Dam. It is a **hydroelectric** dam project near the Gezhouba Dam near Yichang. The Three Gorges Dam will be the *largest* structure ever built when it is completed in 2009. (Ironically, China also has the world's *longest* structure in the Great Wall.)

💡 Why do you think the Three Gorges project is controversial? What does a dam do to the flow of water? Of necessity, the river course is going to have to be maintained and channeled consistently in one direction because of this dam. How could that impact residents right along the river? On the other hand, how could this project positively impact numerous people in China? (Consider not only the resulting electricity generated after the dam's construction but also the number of jobs created by the building project itself.) You can simply discuss these issues, or have older students write responses to these questions. *World* magazine (June 21, 2003, p. 6) had a brief article on the impact this dam is having on local residents. According to the article, 1.3 million people must be relocated to accommodate the dam, and at the point of the article's publication, some 700,000 people had already moved.

🚀 Construct a dam in your sandbox or in a nearby ditch. Use wet sand, rocks, sticks, a board, or whatever other item you wish to build the dam. If possible, have the object creating the blockage penetrable by a screwdriver or some other awl-like tool so *small* amounts of water can be released at one time. Ask your children to observe what happens to the shores of the land behind the dam. (At least two Chinese villages will be completely obliterated by the Three Gorges project.) Also, use this opportunity to explain how hydroelectric power is generated. David Macaulay's *The New Way Things Work* has a simple illustration showing the generating process, using a wheel-and-axle turbine to extract energy from the water moving through the intake pipe.

📺 PBS Home Videos produced a 60-minute film, *Great Wall Across the Yangtze*, specifically on this dam. It investigates the changes this project will bring to China's environment, history, and people.

The Huang He, or Yellow River, is so named because its waters are tinted by its yellow soil. Silt accumulates as the river travels and can raise the riverbed, causing floods or even changing the river's course. Almost all villages and cities in southeast China are located on rivers or canals, which are the equivalent of local highways. **Junks** (ships with quilted sails) and **sampans** (boats with huts onboard) are used for fishing, transportation, and shelter.

✈ Find an origami book that shows how to fold a model junk, or draw a sampan.

Days 5 & 6

⚲ What are some foods common to the area and dependent upon the climate? A crop common to the region is rice, which grows in very wet fields called "paddies," so the monsoon rains and raised river waters can be beneficial for crop success. **Paddies** are water-immersed fields. The flow of water into paddies is carefully controlled to maintain an even depth and temperature in each field. Opening dams in mud banks surrounding the paddies causes water to stream into them. By regulating the speed of the water as it flows through the paddies, farmers can regulate the temperature. Gaps or holes in the mud banks that are made directly opposite each other, cause the water to flow a relatively short distance, keeping the paddy warm, while gaps that are diagonal from each other in the mud banks lengthen the course of the water's flow and cool the water. In northern regions of China, where the climate is not as moist or warm as in the south, making the growing season shorter, another agricultural innovation arose in the form of cultivating the crop in nursery seedbeds of liquid manure. Once the rice shoots grew 5 inches high, they were transplanted to prepared paddy fields (Allison, *Life in Ancient China*, p. 12).

📖 *Everyone Eats Rice*, by Jillian Powell, is a simple book that explains the parts of a rice plant; the known history of rice; how it is grown, harvested, and prepared; and the significance of rice in different cultures.

📖 *Rice Is Life*, by Rita Golden Gelman, is an even more interesting book about the *process* of growing and harvesting rice, but it is set on the island of Bali, below China. That geographical distinction and the difference between a paddy and a *sawah* may confuse some children; still, I think the discussion on the eels, dragonflies, bats, mice, and other critters that are "involved" in rice production is fascinating. *Rice Is Life* also presents another opportunity for thanking our God that He is the one True God to Whom we should express our gratitude for His provision in our lives!

✂ Eat out at a Chinese restaurant, or prepare a traditional Chinese meal. *Cooking the Chinese Way*, by Ling Yu, contains interesting information about regional crops, typical Chinese menus, cooking techniques and utensils, table settings, and basic foods. There is even a listing of Chinese recipe names written in Chinese characters, so your writing students could attempt to create menus for that evening's fare. Of course, it also reminds you how to eat correctly with chopsticks, which is mandatory for such a unit. *Cooking Up World History*, by Patricia Marden and Suzanne Barchers, also provides a variety of recipes (main entrees to desserts) using Chinese fare. In addition, they supply a short annotated listing of other books related to Chinese culture, history, and legend. We in no way advocate all of their supplemental reading suggestions, but they are options you can consider. If you're not an "experimental chef," if you don't think you can afford to buy bamboo shoots and crabmeat, or if you have no Chinese restaurants in your area, at least consider buying rice cakes at the store. (Yeah, those dry, tasteless, circular puffed rice cakes that my

husband claims taste like foam packing peanuts.) Give your children a taste (literally and figuratively) of Chinese life!

⧖ You could also include a discussion of tea facts and history in this section on Chinese foods. For instance, you can relate that tea is served in a covered teacup, which sits on a saucer. The leaves are left in the cup to leach, and the tea is drunk with the cover on to strain the tea leaves (Ferroa, *Cultures of the World: China,* p. 122). When one's cup is refilled with water, it is common to rap one's knuckles on the table three times to indicate thanks. This gesture originated from court officials who once accompanied a Qing emperor traveling **incognito** as a servant. The officials wanted to thank their emperor for refilling their teacups, so they rapped thrice, representing the kowtows of thanks they could not perform. (**Kowtow** is the traditional Chinese way of showing great respect to a superior by kneeling before him and touching one's forehead to the ground.)

❀ Did you know there are 30 types of tea in the world, and they are all found growing in the Yunnan province of China? Most of China's tea grows in the south. Some of the finest teas are found growing on mist-covered cliffs so high up that trained monkeys are used to pluck the leaves. Formerly, Chinese porcelain was shipped to the West in wooden crates filled with tea as a shock absorber. Both items in the crates were then sold at exorbitant prices. And did you know that garlic breath can be eliminated by chewing the tea leaves from one's cup? Apparently, the **chlorophyll** in the leaves will freshen breath.

❀ Another factor to include in any foods discussion is that of proper table manners. In China, it is not considered bad manners to slurp soup at a Chinese table; however, it is poor upbringing if one *chews* noisily. Chopsticks are never to be used as drumsticks on the table, nor are they used to point at a person or gesture during conversation. A meal starts only after everyone is seated, and children respectfully invite their elders to eat before starting their own meals. Usually a mouthful of plain rice is eaten first before other dishes are touched, and a person first helps himself to the nearest dish. Food taken from any dish must be from the part of the plate nearest the person. Moreover, morsels of food must be taken from the top of the serving dish. It is rude to flip over pieces of food or take pieces from the bottom of the plate. And a person never goes for the best pieces; those are reserved for the oldest person or the guest at the table (Ferroa, *Cultures of the World: China,* p. 119).

Day 7

✂ Play games common to China—including mah-jongg (or majiang, based on the idea of the Great Wall of China), *weiqi* ("surround chess"), Chinese checkers, the **tangram** (a square divided into seven pieces, from which numerous pictures are made), pick-up sticks, and kite flying.

You can incorporate historical information here about these different games and activities by reading appropriate portions of a book by Kim Dramer on China from the series *Games People Play!* Did you know, for instance, that kites were used by Chinese military leaders to call troops into action or to spy on their enemies? The decorative design

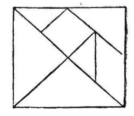

A tangram

of each kite can be of importance, as well, because of certain Chinese folktales and beliefs. Dragons, bats, butterflies, and swallows are among the favorite decorative designs. Again, Demi's *Kites* book will provide more information about the significance of kites in Chinese culture, but I remind you that it comes from an "overly receptive" worldview.

A discussion on Chinese names may be of interest to some students.

> The Chinese name consists of three words: first, the **surname** (the name members of a family have in common), then the generation name, and finally, the given name. The surname is the proudest thing a Chinese child inherits. It is by this name that he or she is known outside the family. The generation name denotes the generation in which a person is born, so often, brothers and male cousins share one name. There are no generation names for girls because the Chinese feel that when girls marry, they belong to another family. Many families now do away with the generation name as parents often have only one child (the politically correct number, according to China's Communist government). Most children today have names consisting only of the surname and the given name, but very careful thought goes into the choice of a name. Parents often choose names that reflect virtues or talents they hope their children will possess (Ferroa, *Cultures of the World: China,* p. 53).

Read *Tikki Tikki Tembo,* by Arlene Mosel, just for fun.

Day 8 (Optional)

View a travel video of China.

Research the martial arts in China.

Taijiquan (also known as Tai Chi), Baguazhang, Xingyiquan, Wu shu, Kung fu, Wing Chun, and Shaolin are among the styles of martial arts taught in China. You may choose to allow your students —older ones, in particular—to research the differences in the varieties of martial arts practiced in China. The could visit a local martial arts studio, interview an instructor, and so forth. I must confess that this is an element of oriental study with which I am a bit uncomfortable. In all of the study I have been able to do on the martial arts, there have been aspects of Eastern mysticism, meditation, and asceticism that do not seem to meld with the Christian faith. In every book I researched, the origins of these physical arts are Buddhist, which sends off mental alarms immediately. Moreover, the martial arts require self-discipline, self-awareness, and a "serious state of mind" (which often equates with a "clearing of the mind," making one's soul all the more susceptible to Satan's wiles). Nevertheless, there are Christian families who have children participating in some form of martial arts without apparent spiritual confusion (and with physical benefits) for their children. Choose what you believe to be best for your family, and for each student in your family.

Chapter 4
Chinese History Lessons

Chinese government existed in the form of dynasties up until the early 20th century A.D. A **dynasty** is a series or succession of rulers from the same line of descent or a powerful group (often a family) that maintains its position for a considerable amount of time. Over the next few weeks we will be learning about 11 of the major dynasties that ruled China. (More than 20 of them existed in their nearly 5,000-year history.) Occasionally, a dynasty may have two or more names listed under its heading; these are simply alternative spellings (or names) for the same dynasty. You may have more success finding resources by using one of the alternative spellings for a dynasty.

The sidebars also provide some brief notes on related or concurrent events and people in history. Hopefully, these introductory notes will help put Chinese history into perspective for families who are maintaining a world history timeline. Timeline figures directly connected with this unit are supplied in Appendix C of *Ancient China: To the Great Wall...and Beyond.* Personally, I am not a huge proponent of memorizing lots of specific dates, but I do think it is important to have a grasp of the general time period or chronological order in which major events occurred and people lived.

Dynasty #1
The HIAH Dynasty
2240–1756 B.C.

Recommended Items
- ❏ Map or globe with Mt. Ararat, Turkey and the Yellow River
- ❏ Bible

Day 1

Noah and Shem

Use Noah timeline figure in Appendix C

Most modern history books refer to the Hsia dynasty as a "legendary" dynasty and do not even begin counting dynasties until the Shang dynasty (see the next section). Yet, most scholars also claim that civilization in this region of the world probably began on the Huang He (Yellow River). Moreover, they acknowledge that an emperor named Yao (or Fohi) ruled from 2240–1998 B.C., and then his son Shin-Nong ruled from 1998–1852 B.C. According to Professor Edward Hull in *The Wall Chart of World History*, Yao was another name for Noah, and Shin-Nong was also known as Shem, Noah's son!

- ❀ Locate Mt. Ararat, Turkey, in relation to the Yellow River on your map.
- ⚲ Review why Mt. Ararat is so significant in Bible history.
    Noah's Ark landed on Mt. Ararat after the Great Flood.

Egyptian dynasties begin around the 20th century B.C.

- 📖 Read Genesis 10:21–31. Where did Noah's sons go after the Flood?
    It is thought that Shem probably settled in Asia, Ham in Africa, and Japheth in Europe. The Great Flood is thought to have occurred between 2348 and 2347 B.C. Noah and his sons then dispersed to settle the earth in 2247 B.C. This time frame would coincide with the chronology of the early Hsia dynasty, yet in spite of these logical conclusions from Biblical and other historical records, many scholars would prefer to believe in Peking man.

Peking Man

Abraham and Lot separate in 1916 B.C.

Some books claim (as Ferroa, *Cultures of the World: China*, p. 17, does) that in December of 1929 the complete skull of a 690,000-year-old **Peking Man** was found in a cave outside Beijing. Some books date this skull even older; *Exploration Into China* (Tao, p. 6) says that Chinese archaeologist, Pei Wenzhong (1904–1982) discovered a 7-million-year-old human skull, which he named "Peking man." Yet, the *Encyclopedia Britannica* on the Internet admits that "Peking man was identified as a new fossil human by Davidson Black in 1927 on the basis of a *single tooth* [emphasis added]." (www.britannica.com; accessed 1/14/03) Is it coincidental or convenient that the fossil evidence disappeared in 1939 just as it was due to be shipped to America for safekeeping? Where the evidence went is one of those "unsolved mysteries" of modern archaeology.

Sodom and Gomorrah are destroyed in 1898 B.C.

- 📖 Read more about this archaeological mystery in *See Through History: Ancient China,* by Brian Williams, p. 44.
- ⧖ Review Biblical history with your children and remind them that the Scriptures in no way support a 7-million-year-old or even 690,000-year-old skull (or *tooth*, for that matter).

13

Dynasty #2
The SHANG Dynasty
1756–1438 B.C.

Recommended Items

- ❑ Bible
- ❑ Bones from butcher
- ❑ Heated poker or wire (optional)
- ❑ Paint and brush for Chinese calligraphy
- ❑ Bronze item from your home
- ❑ Tin and copper samples (optional)
- ❑ Plastic cups for ice molds
- ❑ Silk cloth item from your home
- ❑ Chinese-style dress-up clothes (housecoats, flowing jackets, etc.)

Day 1

Oracle Bones

This is the time of Joseph and Moses, 1700–1500 B.C.

"Oracle" bone inscriptions were the earliest known examples of writing in China. Priests used these bones to answer questions (Hughes-Stanton, *See Inside an Ancient Chinese Town*, p. 30). The Shang kings would consult ancestral spirits on important matters. Ox bones or tortoise shells were scorched until they cracked. The cracks were then "read" to discover the answer to a question posed by the king or priest. Apparently the answers were then inscribed or scratched on the reverse side of the oracle bone. *Ancient China* (*Eyewitness Books* series; Cotterell, p. 11) has a good photo of such oracle bones.

Another source explains that fortune-tellers or diviners used oracle bones to answer the questions of the king. The fortune-teller would drill holes in the surface of a bone and then place a heated rod into each hole; the heat created a pattern of cracks in the bone. These cracks were studied by the fortune-teller, who then scratched (wrote) both the original question and the answer onto the bone (Martell, *Imperial China*, p. 10).

🚀 Break open a turkey or chicken bone (or get a larger bone from your butcher) and attempt to identify the various elements of the bone: marrow, bone cells, fat cells, blood vessels, etc. Use another unbroken bone and a heated poker or wire to replicate the creation of "oracle bones." (**Adult supervision required**.)

⚷ What does the Scripture say about divination? Read Deuteronomy 18:10–14; 2 Kings 17:17–18; Isaiah 47:9–15; and Micah 5:12, for instance. *Vine's Complete Expository Dictionary* explains that the word *qasam* in the Hebrew means "to divine, practice divination" and that it was a "seeking after the will of the gods, in an effort to learn their future action or divine blessing on some proposed future action . . ." (p. 61). Vine's listing elaborates that divination "was one of man's attempts to know and control the world and the future, apart from the true God. It was the opposite of true prophecy, which essentially is submission to God's sovereignty (Deuteronomy 18:14)."

At first only the shamans, or diviners, could read the "magic writing," but many characters or signs like those used in modern writing have allowed experts to read the names of Shang kings (Brian Williams, *See Through History: Ancient China*, p. 7). In 1936, scientists discovered 17,000 of these oracle bones in a single pit. (An extraordinarily curious emperor must have lived in that location, no?)

These early oracle bone symbols or magic writings are also known as the original pictograms.

Day 2

Pictograms

The Chinese written language uses a stylized picture or symbol to represent a word (also known as a character or pictogram), rather than an alphabet of sounds represented by a letter. Combinations of **pictograms** form new meanings or communicate different ideas. For example, two or three tree pictograms may equal "forest" in Chinese writing. Chinese characters, in fact, are sometimes called ideographs, which means "idea-writing." Characters may be made of one to four pictures in combination. Moreover, these images can be arranged in a variety of artistic ways—within the character itself—to create a visually balanced and beautiful idea (Wolff, *Chinese Writing*, p. 15).

The simplest way to write a word, of course, is to draw a picture of the thing it means, while other ideas are conveyed by *combining* characters and symbols. Take, for instance, the word *xiuxi*, which means "rest." *Xiuxi* is formed by four pictograms combined into two shapes—a man, under a tree, resting his eyes, and resting his heart. The word "think" is a combination of the characters for "brain" and "heart." One of the most wonderful pictograms in the Chinese language is for the abstract concept of "to love." The character for "to love" is formed from two noun pictograms meaning "a mother" and her "son."

There are over 70,000 characters today in Chinese writing, though only a few thousand are needed for standard communication. Imagine what one of their typewriter or computer keyboards must look like! Point out to your children that sentences can be written across, left to right, Western-style in modern Chinese. But sentences can also be written in columns, up and down. If it is written in this Chinese-style (up and down), the columns are read from right to left. So the beginning of a Chinese-style book is where Westerners would normally go to find the back or the end.

- ⚲ and ✐ Log on to www.Chinalanguage.com/CCDICT, which allows you to type out English words and see how they appear in Chinese characters. Since your child's name will not be recognized in this Chinese dictionary, why not discover what your child's name *means* and use that for the Chinese translation instead? Have your child attempt Chinese-style calligraphy (using paint and brush) to imitate the character/pictograph that results from your research.

- ⚲ Use the *Hippocrene Children's Illustrated Chinese (Mandarin) Dictionary* to investigate the Chinese characters for your children's favorite toys, colors, or objects. Create several vocabulary cards with a picture of the item, its pronunciation, and its pictogram. Have your child try teaching those words to a friend or a grandparent. The dictionary provides colorful illustrations (from airplane to zebra), pictographs, and pronunciations for a variety of words.

- 📖 Read *Long is a Dragon*, by Peggy Goldstein. It is subtitled "Chinese Writing

The Great Pyramid and the Great Sphinx are built in the mid-1700s B.C.

for Children" and encourages them to practice writing sample characters provided in the book. It also explains pronunciation of Chinese words. You will appreciate how the simple illustration of an idea or a word transitions into the corresponding Chinese pictogram. It helps the ideograph "make sense" visually.

In addition to having a written language, the Shang dynasty is thought to have begun the Bronze Age in oriental culture.

Day 3

Bronze Age

A halberd

The Shang Chinese discovered how to make bronze (an **alloy**, or mixture, of copper and tin). This alloy enabled metalworkers to make bronze weapons, such as spears and **halberds** (ax-like weapons with long wooden handles). Cooking pots called *dings* were also developed during this period. A *ding* was a pot divided inside so that several foods could be cooked at the same time. The first non-electric crockpot, perhaps? The best *dings* were very artistically decorated (Brian Williams, *See Through History: Ancient China*, p. 7).

The Bronze Age in China differed from the European Bronze Age because the Chinese did not make many farming tools. Rather, they concentrated on making bronze weapons and bronze objects for use in their religious ceremonies (Tao, *Exploration Into China*, p. 8). Bronze weaponry was good weaponry, and it is credited with helping the Shang win battles during this time.

Made in China (Suzanne Williams, pp. 6, 7) shows illustrations of how bronze was cast, including the double clay molds—center and outer—used to shape the hot liquid bronze. The center mold was made the size and shape of the pot or item they wanted. Next, sections of soft clay were put over the center mold, forming them to the shape of the outer mold. Designs and words were carved on the inside of the outer mold sections (carved backward, like mirror writing, so that they would turn out right on the finished pot). In order to make room for the bronze, clay was trimmed from the center mold. The outer mold sections were fitted around the center mold and sealed to the outer mold with mud. The bronze then would be poured between the molds like filling between cookies. After the bronze hardened, the outside mold was removed, and the center mold was broken to get it out of the pot.

In later centuries, wax was used to cover the center mold, which could then be carved and decorated as wished. Clay was used to cover the wax model. When the clay hardened, workers poured hot bronze between the two layers of clay. The wax melted and dissipated, which meant the mold was lost. Lost wax pieces were truly one-of-a-kind works of art.

- Get an item of bronze from your home. Let your child feel its weight, coolness, smoothness, and so forth. If you have samples of copper and tin available, let your child feel them and explain that bronze is an alloy that combines those two metals.
- "Reproduce" an early Shang dynasty bronze casting concept by using water inside the mold instead of bronze. We tried using two different sizes of plastic cups for our center and outer molds. Place the mold in the freezer until the

water is hardened (iced) and the cups can be removed. You can even use this "ice" casting for a unique chilled drink on a hot summer day—although we recommend you use it quickly! The difference in cup sizes for the outer and center molds must be fairly great for this ice cup casting to work. We also recommend using disposable plastic cups or cups that you don't care about, just in case the ice splits the cup. (We speak from experience, unfortunately.)

Another unique "invention" attributed to the Shang dynasty was cloth made from silkworm cocoons.

Day 4

Silk

It is not certain when the Chinese first learned to raise silkworms and weave a fine cloth from the threads that make up the silkworm's cocoon, but we know that silk production has been in existence in the Yellow River Valley for more than 4,000 years. A silkworm's cocoon consists of a single strand of silk that may be up to 3,000 feet long. Unwinding a cocoon without breaking the silk thread is a great challenge. To make it easier, each cocoon was soaked or steamed in hot water to loosen the sticky material that held it together (Beshore, *Science in Ancient China*, p. 13). Then sometimes five to eight of those strands were woven together to make a single thread of silk. Talk about a job requiring patience!

📖 Read the simple book *Silk,* by Adele Richardson, which provides more pictures and elementary text to explain silk production.

📖 Lily Hong's young-reader storybook *The Empress and the Silkworm* relates the tale that has been passed down through generations to explain the origins of silk. (It also provides a good opportunity for pointing out the difference in clothing styles and materials among the ancient Chinese classes.)

🚀 Get a silk tie or handkerchief so that your children can handle the cloth, feel the difference in texture, see the fineness in the weave.

✂ Have your child attempt to weave several long strands of hair to get an idea of how delicate and difficult the task of weaving silk thread can be. This is not an easy task at all—particularly if you do not have any family members with long hair.

Just by way of interest, and connected to the idea of silk in some ways, clothing was a sign of class and age in ancient China.

Clothing

Farmers and craftworkers needed clothes that were cheap and practical. The material for these clothes was made from yarn spun from plant fibers. The most common was **hemp**, which was grown on farms in the north and west of the country, but grasses and coarse herbs were also used. Both men and women dressed in a similar style. They wore a short tunic fastened at the waist with a belt, and a pair of trousers that ended just below the knee. Most Chinese, regardless of status, wore similar styles of clothes, in that they wore robes wrapped around and tied at the waist. The robes were in several layers, with the outside layer as the most beautiful. In summer, the layers were thin, and in winter, padding was added between several layers of cloth. Wealthier Chinese also wore stockings

Jason the Argonaut goes exploring in 1268 B.C.

and sandals made from marsh plants or straw (Martell, *Imperial China,* pp. 40, 41). Poor people wore flat shoes or went barefoot.

Wealthy people wore long robes made from expensive silk fabrics that were beautifully decorated. But there were rules about what colors people could wear. For instance, in later eras only the emperor could wear yellow. The emperor and his nobles wore richly decorated silk robes that were too long to run or work in. This was to show that whoever wore those robes did *not* have to work. The scholar and his wife wore less expensive clothes, but their robes were still long, and his shoes had curled toes. Because curled toes are also hard to work or run in, such shoes signified a higher status.

Wealthy women had their feet bound. Cloth strips were wrapped around a girl's feet to bend her toes all the way under to the arches. This literally broke the bones and made the feet like tiny stumps. The foot grew to only about half the normal length. Over time, binding deformed the feet, and made it very difficult for a woman to walk. Nevertheless, small feet were considered delicate and feminine—"lily feet"—and were thought to make a woman more eligible for marriage (Brian Williams, *See Through History: Ancient China,* p. 21). It wasn't until 1902 that an emperor issued an order banning this painful practice!

✂ Attempt to dress in the layers or robes described above. Have a tea party while wearing this Chinese garb, remembering to observe the tea etiquette learned in the geography portion of this unit.

The Shang dynasty was not always "civilized" in its dealing with its citizens. The foot-binding process is testimony to that truth, but even more so were the practices involved in the burial of a Shang ruler.

Day 5 (Please use discretion)

A Shang King's Burial

A Shang king was buried with his treasures and chariots. Also buried around the king's tomb were the actual bodies of animals, human captives, and servants of the king. Human sacrifices were considered an important part of the funeral process. This concept may be too difficult for very tender-hearted children, so please use discretion and God-given wisdom to determine whether or not your child needs to be introduced to this fact at this time.

📖 *See Through History: Ancient China* (Brian Williams, pp. 8, 9) provides more detailed information about this sad ritual. It includes a see-through overlay to explain the burial process.

⏳ Compare and contrast Shang burial rituals with those of the Egyptians from this same basic timeframe by reading a simple book about Egyptian mummies and pyramids, such as *Mummies Made in Egypt,* by Aliki.

Dynasty #3
The ZHOU Dynasty or CHOU Dynasty
1200–282 B.C.

Recommended Items
- ❑ Biography about Confucius
- ❑ Bible
- ❑ Yin and yang illustrations in magazine or clothing catalog
- ❑ Magnet, needle, small plastic foam piece, string, glass
- ❑ Standard directional needle compass (optional)
- ❑ Abacus

Day 1

Feudal Life

Various rulers fought to gain control of the land as emperor. It was during the Zhou dynasty that feudal life really came into existence in China. (By the way, the name of this dynasty, Zhou, is pronounced JOH.) The **feudal system** meant that the land in a region was owned by one ruler, but he made grants of land to nobles in return for their military service. The nobles were lords of their own territories, with absolute rule over their subjects (mostly peasants). They wanted to win and keep the favor of the king, which they usually did by supplying his armies with soldiers, and by fighting the king's enemies. Each noble built castles or walled towns with which to defend his land, with peasants farming the lands and serving as soldiers in the noble's armies. In exchange, the lord protected the peasants in times of attack, and allowed them to keep some of what they produced.

Chinese aristocracy had various ranks, from "dukes" at the top to "barons" at the bottom. Below the noblemen were small landowners and scholars, then farmers and craftsmen, and finally merchants (at least until the Song dynasty, A.D. 960, when the merchant class was elevated to higher esteem in society).

Classes of Society

1. The Shi was made up mainly of nobles and scholars, including poets and philosophers.

2. The Nong was the largest group in Chinese society, made up of peasant farmers and their families. Though poor and often uneducated, they were considered important because they worked hard and provided food for the empire.

3. The Gong was composed of craftworkers—producing beautiful and practical objects of gold, brass, bronze, iron, jade, pottery, porcelain, and lacquerware. Others were carpenters, builders, roof-tile makers, or cart/wagon builders.

4. The Shang was the least respected group during the Zhou period (and is not to be confused with the dynasty of that name); it included merchants and traders. They were often very rich, but even the wealthiest was thought to be less important than the poorest farmer because the merchants produced nothing themselves. They were despised because of this, and many restrictions were put on them.

📖 Read more about these specific classes in Hazel Martell's *Imperial China,* pp. 32–35.

Solomon becomes King of Israel in 973 B.C.

⧗ You may want to point out illustrations of these noblemen and scholars riding in sedan chairs or in rickshaws to acquaint your children with these oriental modes of transportation. A **sedan chair** was an enclosed chair carried on poles by two or four men. A **rickshaw** (or *jinriksha* in its full name) is a small, two-wheeled carriage drawn usually by one person. Remind your children that robes of the Shi class were long, making walking difficult. These two forms of transportation were vital for the noblemen and scholars.

Nebuchadnezzar rules Babylon in 600 B.C.

Day 2

We come to two of the saddest days in our study because millions, if not billions, of people have been blinded by the philosophies of the following individuals. Innumerable well-intentioned souls have believed in something or someone who cannot give them an eternity in Heaven. Please emphasize to your young ones that Jesus died on the cross for *all* men, and that He loves the people of China just as dearly as men from any other country in the world. We need more missionaries to share the truth of the Gospel with the lost and dying souls in China. You can relate the following material in an honest, loving, and humble way without apologizing for your faith and without being condescending about Chinese culture.

Use Confucius timeline figure in Appendix C

Confucius

Religion in China included (and still includes) a variety of influences: ancestor worship, belief in various spirits around the home and countryside, and a mixture of beliefs or philosophies from men like Confucius and Lao Tzu. (Buddhism later was added to this combination during the Han dynasty.)

Confucius is the westernized name for the teacher Kong Qiu, who earned the title Kongfusi (also written as Kung Fu-tzu)—which means the "Great Master Kong." Legend claims that Confucius was born with a hollow in his head, supposedly a storage place for his celebrated wisdom (Allison, *Life in Ancient China*, p. 86). In reality, we *do* know that he was orphaned at an early age. He still managed to get an education based on his family's ties to nobility, and eventually he became a government official who taught moral ethics around 500 B.C. He believed that people are born good and that they have a duty to each other. This duty includes kindness, obedience, respect, courage, sympathy, and sincerity.

💡 How does Confucius's view of mankind's goodness contrast with God's view? See Isaiah 64:6 ("all our righteousnesses are as filthy rags") and Romans 3:12 ("there is none that doeth good, no, not one").

📖 Read a simple biography about Confucius to acquaint your children with his "confused" ideas and philosophies. Please use your God-given discretion, again, in determining whether or not your young child's heart can deal with the falsehoods and spiritual dangers of this man's philosophies.

Confucius's teachings were collected by his followers and became principles for good government and personal behavior. His sayings—such as "If we are not to live with our fellow men, with whom can we live?"—were familiar to all Chinese. In 124 B.C. the Imperial University was set up to teach **Confucianism** to future government officials (Brian Williams, *See Through History: Ancient China*, p. 18). Ironically, although Confucius taught that a person should obey and respect people who are older and more important, the First Emperor of unified China (Shih Huang-Ti in the Qin dynasty) burned Confucius's writings in 212 B.C. because he wanted to make a new start in Chinese rule. Confucius's ideas eventually returned to popularity, nonetheless, particularly in the Han period.

Day 3

Lao Tzu

Use Lao Tzu timeline figure in Appendix C

Another major philosopher and teacher of ancient China was Lao Tzu (or Lao Zi), whose name means "old master." Lao rhymes with "cow," and Tzu is pronounced "Sue." He lived about the same time as Confucius and encouraged people to meditate on the "Tao" (pronounced DOW), or "Way." He claimed that all living things should work together and that man must live in harmony with nature. His ideas about the Tao later became a religion called **Taoism** (Shuter, *The Ancient Chinese*, p. 12). Taoists believe in supernatural beings and practice charms, spells, meditation, and vegetarianism to help them gain "oneness with the universe" and immortality (Ferroa, *Cultures of the World: China*, p. 67). A simple life of meditation, closeness to nature, mysticism, ancient folk religion, prayer, diet, and magic all combined to help believers seek eternal youth (Brian Williams, *See Through History: Ancient China*, p. 19).

♀ According to John 14:6, Who is the *true* Way?

Yin and Yang

The Egyptian dynasty ends in 520 B.C.

The Chinese believed that there was a balance in nature, which came from the idea that there were two forces in everything—two forces called **yin and yang**. Yin was considered weak, passive, female, and dark. Yang was considered strong, active, male, and bright. The two were opposites, but neither could exist without the other (Brian Williams, *See Through History: Ancient China*, p. 19). This concept is represented by the symbol of a circle with interlocking black and white halves. Yin literally means "shaded," and yang means "sunlit." It was generally acknowledged by Chinese that one force usually dominated, while they were both different parts of a single overall force, also called Tao. Human life was an attempt to harmonize these two energies (Allison, *Life in Ancient China*, pp. 79, 80).

Yin and Yang

♀ Observe how the mysticism of Confucianism and Taoism, including the use of symbols like yin and yang, has influenced modern Western culture. Find three examples in magazines, in fashions, or in current events. (*Star Wars* and other space science fiction shows often highlight this philosophy. Skateboarding equipment seems to use the yin and yang symbol frequently. And the modern push for "saving the planet" follows Taoism's ideal of balance with nature, often at the expense of humanity.)

♀ How are the concepts of Confucianism and Taoism compared or contrasted to evangelical Protestantism? What dangers are there in worshiping nature (or "becoming one" with nature) as in Taoism? Are the concepts of yin and yang valid? Would Jesus have been able to exist on earth if this law of nature were truly in effect? Why or why not? Leviticus 11:45 says that we are to be holy as He is holy. There is no combination of good and evil—the so-called yin and yang—in our God!

Day 4

Magnetism and Compasses

It was during the Zhou dynasty that Chinese alchemists noticed that some rocks had a mysterious ability to attract a variety of metal objects. These rocks were called **lodestones**, and by studying lodestones the Chinese observed that they all contained a type of iron ore called magnetite. (A lodestone's attractive force is now called magnetism.) The alchemists also observed that a spoon-shaped piece of lodestone always points in the same direction. Within a few centuries, the alchemists embedded the magnetic rocks in wooden blocks carved in the shape of fish. On cloudy days, when sailors could not determine direction by the location of the sun, they placed the wooden fish in the water to help them figure out which way to sail. Chinese commanders in the army also used these primitive compasses. Later, some 1,300 years ago, the Chinese learned that rubbing a steel needle on a lodestone magnetized the needle as well. Soon they began making compasses that used a magnetized needle (Beshore, *Science in Ancient China*, pp. 21, 22).

Compasses are first mentioned around 1090 B.C. Chinese legend says a Yellow Emperor, God of the Universe, lived in the center of the world. Four other gods ruled the north, south, east, and west, so from the earliest times, Chinese people believed these directions were powerful. The Shang people built walled cities where most doors and graves faced south. The needles on our compasses in North America point north. When you think about it, though, the line of the needle, in fact, points north *and* south. (Does that surprise you?) In China, south was the most important direction, so their compasses pointed south!

- Make your own compass by magnetizing a needle. You will need a steel sewing needle, and you magnetize it by rubbing the head and the tip on a magnet. (Another startling revelation, eh?) You must always rub in the *same* direction on the magnet, some 20 to 30 times. Now, stick the needle through a small centimeter-square piece of plastic foam. Then place your magnetized needle-in-foam in a small bowl or cup filled with water. The needle should float and turn in a north-south manner. By checking the location of the sun, of course, you can then determine which end of the needle is pointing north and which is pointing south. You may want to use a store-bought compass to check the accuracy of your needle compass, just out of curiosity.

- Another variation of this compass construction is the Chinese hanging compass. Again, rub a needle 20 to 30 times on a magnet, rubbing in the same direction so as to magnetize the needle. (Test its magnetism by seeing if the needle can pick up a pin.) Tie one end of a short thread—silk is preferable, of course— around the center of the needle, and the other end around a pencil so that the needle dangles from the pencil. Now place the pencil across the rim of a glass that is wide enough for the needle to move freely. When your needle comes to rest, it should be pointing in a north-south direction.

Mathematics also developed under the Zhou dynasty.

Cyrus of Persia conquers Babylon.

Day 5

Number System

The Chinese invented a system of numbers more than 3,000 years ago. *Science in Ancient China* (by George Beshore) has an entire chapter devoted to this number and math system. Did you know that Chinese mathematicians comprehended the relationship between the diameter (distance across a circle) and the circumference (distance around the outside edge) of a circle? They determined that circumference = pi x radius x radius. It was also during this time that they began using the zero symbol to eliminate confusion in arithmetic solutions. The chart showing the difference between the ancient symbol and the modern symbol for each number is also interesting in this chapter of *Science in Ancient China*.

   📖 *Count Your Way Through China,* by Jim Haskins, teaches children how to count to 10 in Mandarin Chinese, as well as how to write those numbers symbolically.

The Abacus

While it is believed that the Chinese have used abacuses for at least three millennia (placing its use chronologically before the Zhou dynasty), following the number system subtopic would be a perfect time to introduce the abacus to your children. An **abacus** is a hand-operated calculating machine in which numbers are represented by beads strung on wires or rods set in a rectangular frame. The Chinese most commonly use a *suan pan*, meaning "reckoning board." It is an abacus with up to 13 columns of beads divided in two by a bar running across the frame. Each column has two beads above the crossbar and five below it. The far right column represents the "units" column, with each lower bead representing one, and each upper bead representing five. The next column to the left is the "tens" column, then the "hundreds" and so forth. In the "tens" column a lower bead represents 10 and each upper bead 50; in the "hundreds" column a lower bead represents 100 and an upper bead 500. This pattern continues throughout the 13 columns, so a 13-column abacus can register numbers up to 9,999,999,999,999 (Clarke, *The Encyclopedia of How It Works*, p. 7)!

   ✂ Borrow an abacus from your local library or make one of your own. Challenge your child to indicate a given number on his abacus, and then have him attempt simple calculations on the abacus.

Eventually in this dynasty, Zhou kings lost the loyalty of the nobles. In 771 B.C., the then capital city (Hao) was attacked by Mongolian nomad tribes. The Zhou king fled, and in the resulting confusion, the strongest nobles set up their own states. For the next 500 years, warring states battled for power in China. Even so, advancements were made during this warring 500-year period, including the replacement of iron for softer bronze in the making of tools. This also began the period in which bronze coins were introduced for paying taxes to the defeating lord (Brian Williams, *See Through History: Ancient China*, pp. 12, 13).

Alexander the Great "conquers the world."

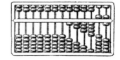

An abacus

a much shorter chapter on the terra-cotta army that could replace the full-length book, although younger students will be intrigued by Lazo's photos of this archaeological dig.

📖 Another shorter book (40 pages) on the topic is *The Emperor's Silent Army*, by Jane O'Connor. The dig is chronicled in simple text and large, color photos.

✄ Use terra-cotta, clay or playing dough to sculpt miniature soldiers or a model Qin house. Time how long it takes to make a miniature soldier, and discuss how long it would possibly take to do a full-size replica. *Marco Polo for Kids*, by Janis Herbert, has a terra-cotta recipe on page 35. It would work perfectly for this activity.

Shih Huang-Ti died at the age of 49. He was buried in a suit made of jade, woven together with knots of gold wire. (See Martell's *Imperial China*, p. 54, for a photo of this jade suit.)

Day 4

Ptolemies I and II reign in Egypt

Jade

Jade is a very hard gemstone that occurs in soft greens, grays, and browns and is satiny smooth when polished. Sometimes it was valued more than gold or silver. Jade was associated with immortality because it was seemingly indestructible, plus the Chinese believed it was vested with magical properties.

An ancient dictionary definition of jade claimed it was "the fairest of stones. It is endowed with five virtues" (Allsion, *Life in Ancient China*, p. 68). The five virtues included charity, morality, wisdom, courage, and justice.

🚐 If you have access to a piece of jade that your student can handle and observe, that would be a wonderful addition to this portion of the study. Now would also be a perfect time to visit a local museum that may have Chinese art made of jade. However, we do not recommend handling the jade objects in the museum! The docents just don't appreciate it.

Dragons

The symbol of the dragon became associated with the First Emperor and was used on his clothing and jewelry. Dragons were actually thought to be benevolent, or helpful, creatures in ancient China. The dragon (called *long*) symbolized wisdom, goodness, and strength, and it represented the life-giving power of water because dragons were thought to live among rain clouds, rivers, lakes, and oceans (Allison, *Life in Ancient China*, p. 70). Isn't it ironic that a domineering, oppressive emperor chose a symbol of benevolence? (Cotterell, *Eyewitness Books: Ancient China*, pp. 16, 17, has detailed photos of dragon images from this time.)

Dynasty #5
The HAN Dynasty
228 B.C.–A.D. 220

Recommended Items
- ❑ CD or cassette tape of Chinese music
- ❑ Bow and arrow
- ❑ Paper "mush"
- ❑ Dryer lint (optional)
- ❑ Simple biography on Buddha
- ❑ Bible

Day 1

While Shih Huang-Ti was feared by his people, he was never really loved. (Recall that families were torn apart or diminished by the forced labor on the Emperor's Great Wall and tomb.) His family did not reign long after his death. Liu Bang, a soldier of humble birth, fought to gain control and became emperor in 202 B.C.; he then took the name Han Gaozu. Incidentally, the Han **ethnic group**—originating around the Yellow, Yangtze and Pearl rivers—remains the largest ethnic group in China and the world (over one billion people). It was during the Han dynasty that China recovered from the First Emperor's difficult rule. Included in this "recovery" was an increased interest in music, farming improvements, the sciences, and papermaking. Buddhism also infiltrated from India during this era.

Roman Republic and Empire exist.

Music

All Chinese music, regardless of the instrument, is based on a musical scale of five tones (rather than the eight tones with which the Western world is most familiar). Han-era ensembles included wind, string, and percussion instruments.

- ♀ Research musical instruments unique to China—including the di-zi (flute), xiou (recorder), ruan (guitar), pipa (lute), yue-qin (mandolin), san-xian (banjo), er-hu (two-string violin), zheng (lap harp), sheng (bamboo mouth organ or pan pipe), and qin (long-bodied zither).

- Web sites offer pictures of these different instruments (see www.chineseculture.net) and samples of Chinese music (see www.bigskymusic.com). Draw a picture of the most unique Chinese instrument you have encountered in your research.

- ♪ Listen to Chinese music, which is based on a five-tone scale instead of the eight-tone system with which Westerners are most familiar. *Chinese New Year Celebration Music*, by Kimbo Educational, is a cassette tape that includes four simple songs—some using familiar tunes, some using traditional oriental tunes. The four songs convey the importance of music, activity, and celebration in the Chinese New Year. These are suited mainly for K–3 students in terms of simplicity, but no judgment is made about Chinese astrology or dragon praising, so please be forewarned! *Music and Menus: China*, by Intersound Entertainment, provides two compact discs of music, and a booklet of menu

A Cheng or mouth organ

suggestions for a Chinese dinner. The first disc contains music with the five-tone oriental sound, including songs with names like "The Red Azalea" and "Washing Silks by the River." The second disc contains songs that use the eight-tone scale but include a Chinese theme in their words or style, such as "The Chinese Dance" from *The Nutcracker* or highlights from *The Mikado* and *Madame Butterfly*.

🚐 Take a field trip to a community college or university in your area for a concert of Chinese music.

Day 2

Building Construction

See Inside an Ancient Chinese Town, by Penelope Hughes-Stanton, is an excellent way to gain greater insight into the culture and history of the Han dynasty. Learn about the true town of Loyang (also spelled Luoyang), along the Lo River. It was an impressively fortressed city, and well organized in its civic design.

Brian Williams' *See Through History: Ancient China*, pp. 24, 25, provides an overlay depiction of a nobleman's house from the Han period. Construction was usually of wood, which was preferred over stone because it was considered more "natural." (Review Taoism's influence and the concept of yin and yang in life.) A wooden house was also less likely to harm its residents during an earthquake. These homes often had overhanging eaves that were curved, allegedly to please the house spirits as well as to provide shade from the sun.

Farming Improvements

Improvements in farming during the Han dynasty included the invention of the wheelbarrow, which originally had one large wheel rising through the center of its base that allowed the weight to be lifted more easily (Cotterell, *Eyewitness Books: Ancient China*, p. 23). Irrigation systems were also developed to regulate the water supply to crops. Rice paddies in northern China were frequently located on narrow hillside terraces (making the most of the limited land for planting). Water was raised to the terraces by irrigation machines powered by humans—such as the "endless chain" machine, which used pedals turning a cogwheel that was connected to an endless chain of wooden paddles that pulled a stream of water uphill. (See Cotterell's *Eyewitness Books: Ancient China*, pp. 34, 35, for models; Shuter's *The Ancient Chinese*, p. 26, for a painting; and Suzanne Williams's *Made in China*, p. 10, for a better textual explanation of these irrigation machines.)

✈ Older students may want to attempt a model of the endless chain irrigation machine using balsa wood or even paper cups.

Day 3

Crossbows

Another invention of note during the Han dynasty included the crossbow (Suzanne Williams, *Made in China*, p. 13). It could be pulled tighter, aimed better, and shot farther than regular bows. Some crossbows were large enough that a team of men was needed to load the arrow and pull the bowstring. The triggering system for releasing the bowstring was the most unique feature of the crossbow.

Julius Caesar's wars in France and Britain occur between 58 and 49 B.C.

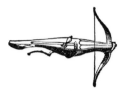

A crossbow

✂ Shoot a traditional bow and arrow, and then discuss the difference in aiming and shooting a crossbow. If you have access to a crossbow, this activity will be even more enriching. **Adult supervision in this activity,** *please*!

Seismographs

Chang Heng (mathematician, astronomer, and civil servant) invented a seismographic machine in A.D. 132. It could not measure how strong an earthquake was, as do the **seismographs** of today, but it could indicate the quake's direction from the capital, Loyang. It could even alert officials to small or faraway earthquakes that they could not feel. The original machine was bronze and measured 6 feet across. It had eight balls in the mouths of eight dragons around the outer edge of the apparatus. When a column in the middle of the machine vibrated during an earthquake, it caused one of the eight dragon heads to drop a ball into the mouth of a frog that sat below. The dragon without a ball in its mouth usually pointed to the direction of the earthquake.

📖 *Made in China*, by Suzanne Williams, provides a photograph of the apparatus and a more detailed explanation of the machine (p. 25).

Day 4

Paper

It was during the Han dynasty that the cumbersome bamboo books (thin bamboo strips held together in a bundle) of previous dynasties were replaced by actual paper books. The process of papermaking included soaking bamboo, hemp, or mulberry bark. A mold called a screen was then dipped into the mushy pulp and gently shaken until the fibers settled onto it. Then the screen was pressed to remove the water from the pressed pulp before being left to dry (Cotterell, *Eyewitness Books: Ancient China*, p. 24, and Allison, *Life in Ancient China*, p. 68). Consider how papermaking increased the availability of reading material, which increased literacy among the general population, as well. By the way, papermaking in Europe did not occur until A.D. 1150, approximately 1,050 years later.

✂ Attempt the process of making paper from mushy pulp. The Boy Scouts of America has a book entitled *Pulp and Paper*, by T.J. Stenuf, which explains the process fairly simply. A slightly more extravagant and creative form of papermaking is presented in Marianne Saddington's *Making Your Own Paper*. You may want to save dryer lint from the lint trap and use that instead of mushy pulp to make a more linen-like paper. Please save some of this paper for a later activity during the Tang period.

It was also during the Han dynasty that a "third way" of grappling with life and death was absorbed into the Chinese culture in the form of Buddhism.

Day 5

Buddhism

Use Buddha timeline figure in Appendix C

Buddhism filtered its way east from India during the Han dynasty, when the emperor sent for copies of Buddhist writings. Actually, Buddhism and Taoism had much in common. Both asserted that everlasting life could be achieved through self-discipline and meditation.

Chinese emperors even employed Buddhist counselors as political advisors because of their apparent wisdom and for their supposed magical skills (Brian Williams, *See Through History: Ancient China,* p. 19).

📖 Read a simple biography on Buddha, remembering to counteract the hopelessness of his philosophies with the truths of Scripture.

☍ Older students can research who Buddha was and give a brief oral report on his life and teachings.

Buddha was an Indian prince named Siddhartha Gautama, who devoted his life to searching for personal peace and enlightenment. When Siddhartha was 29 years old, he gave up his life of luxury and wealth because he was so unhappy. For the next 44 years, he searched for enlightenment. (The name *Buddha* actually means "enlightened one.") Buddha claimed that by denying oneself worldly desires—including fine food and clothes—a state of **Nirvana** could be reached. In nirvana there was supposedly freedom from this world's sorrows. Reincarnation was also a key aspect to Buddhist thought. People were reborn many times, and those who had lived badly in former lives might be reborn in animal or insect form. Buddha said that by reaching nirvana, the endless cycle of rebirth would be broken.

☍ Find a Bible verse or passage that disproves the concept of reincarnation (Ecclesiastes 3:2 and Hebrews 9:27). Now find a passage that reveals Jesus as the *truly* Enlightened and enlightening One (John 1:4–9).

📖 Demi's book *Kites* reveals the wide variety of Buddhas that were incorporated into Chinese society—a Buddha for wisdom, peace, overcoming ego, etc. Again, aren't we grateful for one True God?

Some of these concepts are going to be difficult for younger students, yet I think it is important that we contrast the images of the various Buddha idols with the image of Christ hanging on a cross. Buddhism and China's other false religions are such futile religions, offering little to no hope for a better future, but there *is* hope in the Way, the Truth and the Life when one trusts in Jesus Christ as one's personal Savior. Again, we must be careful that we don't come across as "bashing" Chinese culture; rather, we simply desire to point out how blinded man has become to the true Gospel. Haunting photos of various Buddhist idols in *China* (by Zheng Shifeng) reveal the influence that Buddhism still has on China. At the end of the Han regime (third century A.D.), Taoist sects rose up against the Han government and led to its collapse. Taoists in the sects often wore yellow turbans around their heads, so their uprisings have been called the Yellow Turban Rebellions. From the early A.D. 300s to 580, power struggles continued until the rise of the Sui dynasty.

Dynasty #6
The SUI Dynasty
A.D. 589–618

Recommended Items
- ❑ Pictures of pagodas
- ❑ Small ditch and wood pieces for canal with locks

Day 1

The first Sui emperor, Yang Chien, reunited China after these years of conflict and rebellion by cutting the taxes and by shortening the period of **conscription** (forced time of service in the army). It was during his rule that Buddhism's influence in Chinese culture became even more pronounced.

Pagodas

It was during the Sui dynasty that pagodas appeared in China. **Pagodas** are Far Eastern towers, often used as Buddhist libraries or places of worship, and usually having roofs that curve upward at the division of each story. Some of the first pagodas were built by Chinese monks in imitation of temples they had seen in India. Extra stories were sometimes added to these pagodas over the centuries.

➤ Philip Steele's *Step Into the Chinese Empire*, on pages 16 and 17, has a project for making a model of a pagoda—not that most homeschoolers would want one in their homes! But the option is there, nonetheless.

Pagoda tombs in the county of Denfeng (province of Henan) are outside the Shaoling Temple; since there are about 220 pagoda tombs there, it is sometimes called the Pagoda Forest. When a monk of the temple dies, his remains are assigned to a pagoda tomb whose height and number of stories correspond to his Buddhist learning and position.

📖 Great photos of various pagodas are found in Zheng Shifeng's *China*, pp. 74, 184, 199, 202. Some of these structures really are imposing works of architecture.

Day 2

The Grand Canal

Emperor Yang Chien also encouraged agriculture by setting up irrigation systems so that more rice and grains could be grown, making the country strong again. But it was under the rule of the second Sui emperor, Yang Di, that the Grand Canal was rebuilt on a large scale. The canal had been started in the fourth century B.C. to link the then capital of Loyang to the old capital of Xian, but it was gradually increased to join Hangzhou in the south with Beijing in the north. It is the oldest and longest man-made canal in China (if not the world). In terms of the immensity of the project, it was on a scale with the Great Wall of China. It is 1,114 miles long and connects the Huang He (Yellow), Yangtze, Huai, and Qiantang rivers. Canal travel made it possible to journey from the south to the north without having to use the dangerous sea route or the time-consuming roads. The canals also became a major way of transporting food from the fertile south to the barren north

Pope Gregory I sends Augustine to convert the Anglo-Saxons to Christianity.

Augustine lands in England with 30 missionaries; he appears at Kent and converts King Ethelbert I and his people to Christianity.

Japan has its first written constitution.

and of mobilizing troops in time of war (Ferroa, *Cultures of the World: China*, p. 11).

See Through History: Ancient China (Brian Williams, pp. 32, 33) uses overlay illustrations to show the process of moving ships through canals. Chinese engineers dug canals on level ground, making few differences in water levels. Approximately every 3 miles a flash-lock would be constructed, which was essentially a sluice gate that used a log to stop or control the water flow. To change levels along the canal, boats were hauled by windlass up the two-sided slipway. It was a precarious process, and a boat could be easily damaged if it toppled over the top of the slipway. Later, in the 10th century, the pound-lock was developed; it had gates at each end and could be emptied or flooded as needed in order to raise and lower the boats between levels.

> Construct a canal (in miniature, of course) with the different styles of locks, and observe how water levels rise and lower differently with each style of lock.

Yang Di, the second Sui emperor, also built palaces and pleasure parks for himself by commanding the people to pay taxes 10 years in advance. (And you thought our *current* taxes were awful.) It is no surprise that the peasants rebelled in 618, killing Yang Di. Li Yuan, a Sui official, then founded the Tang dynasty.

Muhammad supposedly has his vision in which the Archangel Gabriel commands him to proclaim the one true god, Allah.

Dynasty #7
The TANG Dynasty
A.D. 618–906

Recommended Items
- ❏ Unfired pottery vase, plate, or terra cotta planter
- ❏ Pottery paint
- ❏ Tea
- ❏ Paper for lantern project
- ❏ Paper and scissors or single-edge razor for papercut project
- ❏ Fireworks (optional)

Day 1

No, Tang had nothing to do with the imitation orange juice drink popularized in the 20th century by the men and women of NASA. The Tang dynasty was a time of excellence in the arts, science, and technology. Printing presses from the 10th century used wooden blocks in which the pictures and text were carved in reverse of the final printed copy. The carving was a laborious process, but many copies could then be printed from one block, versus duplicating every copy by hand.

Poetry

This increased ability to print works also encouraged poets of the period to write even more. Some of the great poets of the time were Wang Wei, Li Po, and Du Fu.

📖 and ♀ *Exploration Into China*, by Tao, p. 21, contains two samples of the poetry from this period. Or log on to www.Chinapage.com/poetry9.html for more examples of poetry, some of which can even be heard in Chinese.

Chinese poetry often uses images from the world of nature to set the mood. Feelings and emotions are expressed through the natural elements described. One of the major themes of these works is the impermanence of human life and relationships (Allison, *Life in Ancient China*, p. 71). Below are some examples of Tang poetry:

> Day after day we can't help growing older.
> Year after year spring can't help seeming younger,
> Come let's enjoy our winecup today.
> Not pity the flowers fallen!
> "On Parting with Spring" by Wang Wei

> The autumn hills hoard scarlet from the setting sun.
> Flying birds chase their mates,
> Now and then patches of blue sky break clear—
> Tonight the evening mists find nowhere to gather.
> "Magnolia Hermitage" by Wang Wei

> All the birds have flown up and gone;
> A lonely cloud floats leisurely by.
> We never tire of looking at each other—
> Only the mountain and I.
> "Alone Looking at the Mountain" by Li Po

Muhammad begins dictating the Koran, the holy book of Islam.

The Byzantine empires rise.

33

✎ Write four lines of your own Chinese-style poetry. Remember to combine the ideas of scenes in nature with personal emotions. Save this poem because you can use it with another project (in the Song dynasty) involving watercolor painting!

Mandarins

Incidentally, every educated person of this period could write both prose and poetry, and it was even a part of the examination to get a job in local government. These civil service exams issued during the Han and Tang dynasties determined whom the governing officials would be. A member of this new ruling group was called a **mandarin**. Mandarin actually comes from a Portuguese word used to denote any member of the imperial Chinese government. There were nine grades of rank in this civil service group.

🖌 Color a picture of mandarin fashions. Dover Publications produces the *Chinese Fashions Coloring Book,* by Ming-Ju Sun, which supplies images covering over 1000 years of fashion, from the Tang dynasty to the Republic period (1911-1949). Men's and women's fashions, as well as hairstyles, are presented. Some explanation is also provided on the common symbols, fabric choices, and key fashion influences in the different dynasties. Students may enjoy coloring a sample of the fashions for each of the remaining dynasties to add to their portfolios of work. This also makes a great reference tool for the families that enjoy dressing in period costume while studying a particular era of history.

Day 2

Porcelain

Porcelain, fine pottery, was also developed during the Tang period to a more advanced degree than it was in the Han dynasty. It was made from special fine white clay, which was fired or baked at very high temperatures. (It's actually a cross between glass and pottery.) For many centuries the Chinese alone knew how to make porcelain because families only passed their secrets on to sons. The secrets were about the clay, firing temperatures, mixing glazes or glass-like paint, and the art of painting objects inside vessels in such a way that they are visible only when the vessel is filled with liquid! The wrong heat could make a piece turn dark, or the wrong amount of iron, copper, or cobalt in a glaze could change the piece's color. It is interesting that travelers were not even allowed to stay overnight in Kingtechen, a town where the emperor's porcelain was made, for fear that the porcelain-making secrets would be discovered (Haskins, *Count Your Way Through China,* #8).

📖 Suzanne Williams in *Made in China,* p. 43, explains the process in even more detail, particularly for the fine porcelain of the Song and Ming dynasties.

🖌 Paint a pottery plate or vase, imitating the natural patterns that were often used in Chinese porcelain work. It would be wonderful if you had access to an actual pottery kiln to fire the final product and experiment with the effect of overheating the kiln or letting the piece stay in the kiln too long to see how such actions change the finish.

✂ Have a tea party using porcelain cups and eating rice cakes.

Islam's empire grows to include Jerusalem, Constantinople, Pakistan, and more.

Lacquerware

Another art form unique to China, lacquerware derives from the sap of the lac tree, a kind of oak tree. In the Tang dynasty, the sap was used for making boxes, bowls, sword sheaths, shields, and coffins. The surface was good for painting and engraving. Most painters favored red, green, yellow, and blue colors, with designs from nature (birds, fish, flowers, and clouds among the favorites). Lacquerware was constructed by using a wood or fabric core for the base, then applying base and top coats of lacquer. Natural lacquer is gray, but pigment could be added to it to make it black or bright red. The surface could then be painted; lastly, the entire item was polished and buffed until the lacquer shone. Or the lacquer could be applied in many layers until it was thick enough to be carved and inlaid with mother-of-pearl.

Day 3

Another form of entertainment and artwork that developed during the Tang dynasty was paper art, in the forms of paper lanterns and papercuts.

Lanterns

The Lantern Festival began during the Tang dynasty. Paper lanterns are hung soon after the New Year to mirror the first full moon of the year. Many homes still decorate their porches with these colorful lanterns.

>✂ Make your own Chinese lantern following the instructions in Philip Steele's *Step Into the Chinese Empire,* pp. 60 and 61.

Papercuts

Papercuts are a common person's art form in China. The materials are basic: a piece of paper and a pair of scissors. A few random snips of the scissors or precise cuts following a design in one's imagination, and a work of art is formed. Patterns can be symmetrical, repeated patterns, or complicated designs with birds, animals, flowers, or popular opera characters. Amazingly elaborate papercuts are still used to decorate the house during festive seasons such as the Spring Festival (Ferroa, *Cultures of the World: China,* p. 90).

>✂ Create your own papercut design. You will need colored paper, pencil, ruler, and scissors. Take a piece of paper and lay it flat on a hard surface. Fold it exactly in half horizontally. Make a firm crease along the fold. Draw a Chinese-style design on the paper. Make sure all the shapes meet up at the fold. Keeping the paper folded, cut out shapes. Be certain you don't cut along the entire folded edge and cut away areas you want to discard in between the shapes. Now carefully open your design, and display the finished cutout by sticking it to a window or attaching it to your Chinese lantern, so that light shines through the pattern! (This basic process is taken from Steele's *Step Into the Chinese Empire,* p. 46.)

Charlemagne is pronounced the Holy Roman Emperor in 800.

Day 4

Gunpowder

It's ironic that, in an age of such beauty and poetry, gunpowder was invented. **Gunpowder** is a mixture of charcoal, sulfur, and saltpeter that explodes when heated. It was invented accidentally (and ironically) by a scientist/alchemist who was trying to make a potion to give everlasting life (the elixir of life). By the 10th century, this elixir was used for making fireworks (which were initially used simply to scare enemies in battles), then weapons like rockets, guns, bombs, and mines. (See George Beshore's *Science in Ancient China*, pp. 19–21, for more details on these stages of development.) These weaponry developments allowed the Tang empire to grow in size because other lands and nations could be more easily conquered.

- Tour a fireworks factory.
- Take apart a firework to see its components. **This firework dissection should only be done under strict adult supervision!** Or read David Macaulay's *The New Way Things Work* to learn how a rocket/firework is put together and propels upward.
- PBS/NOVA has produced a sixty-minute program entitled *Fireworks!* that also provides an excellent discussion of the history of fireworks, how different types of fireworks are produced, and what goes into modern-day fireworks displays. This program is usually shown on PBS around the Fourth of July, or you may find it available in video format through your library's interlibrary loan system.

Cities in North America apparently are established during this period.

Dynasty #8
The SONG *Dynasty*
A.D. 960–1279

Recommended Items
- ❏ Homemade paper from Han dynasty project
- ❏ Poem from Tang dynasty project
- ❏ Blankets to make a yurt
- ❏ Large paper for "wanted" poster
- ❏ Book of Mongolian costumes
- ❏ Reservations at a Mongolian restaurant (optional)

Day 1

Following the Tang dynasty, five different emperors in 53 years tried to reunite China and start new dynasties, but none of them were successful. Finally, the first Song emperor came to the throne in 960, although his empire was smaller than that of previous dynasties.

There were a number of developments during this period.

The "Three Perfections"

Painting, poetry, and calligraphy were considered the three perfections, that is, the height of artistic expression, particularly from the Song dynasty (960–1279) onward. It was considered to be the greatest accomplishment of an educated person to combine the form of a poetically inspired landscape painting with beautiful calligraphy running down one side of the picture (Cotterell, *Eyewitness Books: Ancient China*, p. 31). Paintings developed on silk, paper, and bamboo. Scenes for these paintings included court life, busy streets, village life, industry, and farming. Gardens and natural scenes were also thought of as works of art and were favorite places for poets to sit and write, especially during the Tang dynasty (Martell, *Imperial China,* pp. 55, 56).

A calligrapher or painter from this dynasty would have possessed a large collection of brushes. A professional calligrapher might need a brush with bristles or hairs more than a foot long for writing big characters on posters and banners (Cotterell, *Eyewitness Books: Ancient China,* p. 33).

In the eyes of the Chinese, writing was as important for its own beauty as for the message it contained. Calligraphy, or the art of writing Chinese characters, was done with brushes dipped in ink. "Chinese words make sense to the eye…The essence of calligraphy is movement, balance, flow, energy. Not the *meaning* of the character, but the *way* it is written is important" (Wolff, *Chinese Writing*, p. 21).

🖌 Take the paper you made during the Han dynasty. Use two different colors of watercolor—one for the sky, one for the earth. Paint each horizontal half of the paper with those two respective colors. Now use other watercolors to paint something from nature; try a single tree branch or grouping of flowers, for instance. Let it dry thoroughly. Then try using a calligraphic handwriting style (even using a brush with ink, if you dare) to rewrite your poem from the Tang dynasty lessons onto this "Three Perfections" exercise.

Eric the Red, the Viking, sets out from Iceland and lands on Greenland.

37

The final break between the Byzantine Empire and the Roman Church takes place; the Eastern Orthodox Church becomes completely independent (1054).

Day 2

The arts were not the only advances made during the Song regime. Science advanced in terms of its accomplishments in astronomy and medicine.

The Astronomical Clock

Su Song built the first mechanical clock that told the time of day and tracked the stars and planets so that "more accurate" horoscopes could be drawn. The clock was driven by the flow of water into the buckets on a waterwheel. Each bucket filled to tilt a lever, then the next bucket advanced. The clockwork was housed in a large tower. Revolving figures appeared at windows of the tower to chime the hours (Suzanne Williams, *Made in China*, p. 33). There was also an inside platform housing a celestial globe, and an **armillary sphere** for monitoring celestial objects was located on the roof of the tower.

Often in discussions of life in China, particularly around the New Year, one will hear the comment, "This is the year of the Rat (or the Pig, the Tiger, etc.)." Students may be curious as to what this animal reference is about, so I've included a brief discussion on the Chinese zodiac. Again, the One Who made the stars is in control of man's life; the stars have no influence on mankind's destiny (Amos 5:8; Job 9:6–10 and 38:31–33). Please determine for yourself if your student is mature enough spiritually for this material. May we never confuse our children's faith by our study of any other religion or event in history before they are spiritually ready to handle such information!

Chinese Zodiac

According to legend, on his deathbed Buddha summoned all the animals of the kingdom to his bedside. Only 12 of the animals decided to show up, and in the order of their appearance Buddha dedicated a year to each of them. The Chinese zodiac moves in a cycle of 12 years. Supposedly, people born under these signs possess certain characteristics, as listed below.

The Battle of Hastings takes place in 1066. William of Normandy declares himself king of England.

Rat	1984, 1996	Charming, ambitious, and thrifty
Ox	1985, 1997	Steadfast, methodical, and stubborn
Tiger	1986, 1998	Dynamic, short-tempered, and powerful
Rabbit	1987, 1999	Humble, artistic, and clear-sighted
Dragon	1988, 2000	Flamboyant, talented, and lucky
Snake	1989, 2001	Discreet, intense, deep, and intelligent
Horse	1990, 2002	Popular, competitive, and independent
Sheep	1991, 2003	Artistic, creative, and religious
Monkey	1992, 2004	Witty, discriminating, and good-humored
Rooster	1993, 2005	Aggressive, hardworking, and a perfectionist
Dog	1994, 2006	Honest, loyal, and cooperative
Pig	1995, 2007	Caring, studious, and home-loving

What credibility does the zodiac have for you as a Christian? What does the Bible say about searching the stars for life's answers? (Isaiah 47:9–13)

Day 3

Medical Advances

During the Song dynasty, acupuncture, moxa, antiseptics, and vaccinations were common medical practices in China. Chinese doctors believed that if one was experiencing pain or illness, it was because the balance between yin and yang—the two opposing forces of life—was somehow disrupted. It was the doctor's duty to restore the balance between yin and yang in the patient's body.

Acupuncture is a form of traditional Chinese medicine in which needles are inserted at certain points or nerve centers along the body to relieve pain or cure certain diseases. The Chinese believed that acupuncture affected the flow of *chi*, which is the life force that flows through one's body. Bone needles were first used but then were replaced by bronze and copper needles. Acupuncture is still in use today, particularly to relieve arthritis, asthma, migraine headaches, ulcers, and eye troubles (Beshore, *Science in Ancient China*, p. 27). It is thought that the needles temporarily, at least, interrupt the transmission of pain messages through the nervous system.

Moxa (also known as **moxibustion**) treats patients by stimulating specific sites along the body with heat instead of needles. Small cones, dried leaves, or sticks of wormwood were placed at various points along the body and set on fire. The ashes were then rubbed into the blisters that formed on the skin. It was a procedure used to treat mainly chronic or long-lasting illnesses.

Antiseptics were used as early as 980 during an epidemic when a Chinese monk, Tsan-Ning, advised people to steam the clothes and bedding of sick people so that other family members would not become ill. (This antiseptic process prevented the growth of germs.)

In the year 1000, Chinese scientists and doctors had developed a vaccination to prevent people from becoming infected by the smallpox virus. (Edward Jenner of England did not discover his vaccine for this virus until 1796!) A **vaccination** is the introduction of a small amount of a virus so that the body will develop immunities to that virus.

   📖 Read more about these medical advances in Beshore's *Science in Ancient China*.

Days 4 & 5

Mongol Invasion

In 1068, Prime Minister Wang Anshi, reformed government by simplifying taxes and by cutting down the huge army to a more reasonably sized fighting force. While these cuts saved money, they also made it easier for foreigners to invade China, especially from the north, which is what happened under Temujin and his Mongol hordes. He began invading the country in 1190, and the Great Wall offered little protection against these nomadic warriors. By 1206, Temujin officially became Genghis Khan, which means "Emperor of All Men."

The first Crusade begins in 1096. Volunteers are requested by the Pope to free the Christian holy places in Palestine from the Muslims. The last Crusade is in 1291.

Archbishop Becket quarrels with King Henry II in England over the Church's rights; Becket is murdered eight years later.

Use Genghis Khan timeline figure in Appendix C

Mongols were soldiers who struck fear into all of Asia and west into Europe. The Mongols were considered "barbarians" by the Chinese, but they controlled most of northern China by 1220, and were invading Russia, Persia (now Iran), and Iraq by 1258. It's interesting to note how key the remarkable horsemanship and sheer terror of the Mongols was in allowing them to conquer the territory. The Mongols attacked on horseback, and were seemingly tireless warriors. They could ride for 10 days without eating or resting; when they became weak for lack of food, they would cut veins in their horses' legs and drink the blood for strength. When the Mongols captured a town, they would enlist the town's men into their army (on threat of killing those who didn't join), and then push on to take over the next town.

- The Mongols lived in tent-like domed dwellings called **yurts**. Design your own yurt from chairs and blankets.

- Take a flashlight into your yurt and read a chapter of *Genghis Khan and the Mongol Horde*, by Harold Lamb. If you are unable to read the entire book because of the young age of your children (and the wiggles that accompany youth), read Chapters 8 and 9 to introduce your children to the Khan's domination of Cathay.

- If possible, continue reading more of the Landmark book *Genghis Khan and the Mongol Horde* while your students draw and color an illustration of what a Mongol's fashions may have been like. Use *Mongol Costumes*, by Henny H. Hansen, to draw these pictures. Or refer to Ming-Ju Sun's *Chinese Fashions Coloring Book* for fashions from this era.

- Design a wanted poster for Genghis Khan.

- If you can afford it and there is one near you, try eating out at a Mongolian restaurant. Some restaurants of this nature even serve the food in "hats" or bowls similar to the helmets Mongolian warriors wore.

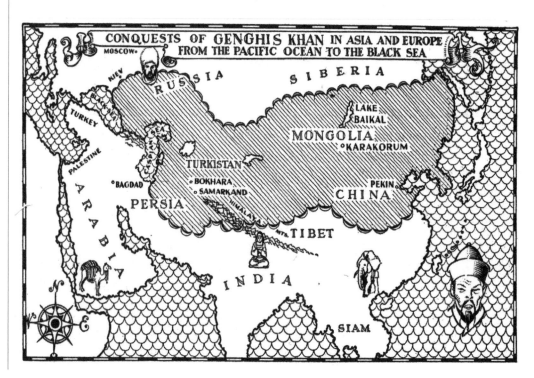

Dynasty #9
The YUAN Dynasty
A.D. 1279–1368

Recommended Items
- ❑ Reproducible map of Eurasia in Appendix C
- ❑ Magazines for cutting out collage pictures
- ❑ Drawing materials
- ❑ Copy of Samuel T. Coleridge's poem "Kubla Khan"
- ❑ Video or DVD or the Khan's summer palace, Xanadu (optional)

Day 1

The last Song emperor died in 1279. By then, the conquering Genghis Khan's heir, Kublai Khan, had taken control and established Beijing (Peking) as his capital city. Kublai Khan and his rulers, the Yuan, controlled China until 1368. Since the Yuan were themselves foreigners, they sometimes had foreign officials working for them—which explains Marco Polo's influence during Kublai Khan's regime.

Silk Road

The **Silk Road** was in existence from about 100 B.C., stretching some 2,500 miles and linking the Han and Roman empires when both were at their peak. This road continued to be an important trading route during the Yuan dynasty. Caravans of camels took silk from China across the deserts and mountains to the shores of the Black Sea. There the silk was traded for Western luxuries, and then the silk was taken across the Mediterranean Sea to Greece and Rome. The most popular route of the Silk Road crossed the Gobi desert, Bactria, and Seleucia before reaching Rome. At this time, the only other practical way of trading goods with the West was by sailing the Spice Route, which involved sailing from China and the Spice Islands, over the Indian Ocean to the Red Sea and the Persian Gulf. Point out the dangers faced during these long treks, regardless of which mode of transportation one took. On the sea, ship travel was hazardous and dependent upon the elements. Across the land, thieving nomads, desert windstorms, lack of water, and rugged mountains created difficulties in travel.

Robert the Bruce becomes King Robert of Scotland in 1328 after England acknowledges Scotland's independence.

- ✸ Chart the most frequently used route for the Silk Road on your Eurasia map. *Marco Polo: A Journey Through China*, by Fiona Macdonald, provides a simple map of this road. Or *The Travels of Marco Polo*, by Marion Koenig, provides a more detailed, city-by-city map of the route.
- ⚲ Research **Bactrian camels**. How do they differ from other camels in their genus (*Camelus*)? How are they different from dromedaries, for instance? What are their unique features, and why were they so beneficial to Silk Road travels?

    Bactrian camels have two humps instead of one (as the dromedary has), making them more comfortable for riding. They survive the cold winter temperatures in the deserts of central Asia by growing an extra-thick coat of fur in the fall. Most Bactrian camels are now domesticated, and most live in Mongolia or China.

One of the most memorable characters ever to travel the Silk Road was Marco Polo.

Days 2-4

Use Marco Polo timeline figure in Appendix C

Marco Polo

Born in Venice, Italy, in 1254, Marco Polo was the son of a trader who had already made one trip to China and back. The elder Polo and his brother (Marco's uncle) had promised the Kublai Khan that they would return with Christian missionaries to train the Khan's people in Christianity. (Christianity was equated with Catholicism at this point.) The Pope refused to send the hundreds of missionaries the Khan had requested, but the Polos returned to China regardless. Marco Polo was only 17 years old in 1271 when the Polos again headed east to the Khan's territory. For the next 20 years of his life, he remained in China studying their ways and culture, learning their languages, and noting interesting facts and inventions. The Khan trusted Marco Polo because of his knowledge of the different languages under the Khan's rule and because of his honest answers to even the most difficult of questions. Marco was made a commissioner who was sent out to observe and inspect the different countries of the Mongolian empire. Finally, in 1292 the Polos returned to Italy, much to the surprise of family and friends. Initially, the Venetians did not believe the stories the Polos told of their experiences with the Khan. When the Polos revealed jewels they had hidden in the linings of their tattered garments, their stories were more readily accepted. (Or was it their wealth that was more readily accepted?) Marco Polo was imprisoned in 1298, however, when Venice and Genoa went to war. In prison, a writer named Rustichello of Pisa recorded Marco's tales and descriptions, which were then published as a book, *The Travels of Marco Polo, the Venetian*. It soon became a bestseller and still contains remarkable descriptions of life in China under the Kublai Khan's reign.

- 📖 For younger readers, *Marco Polo: A Journey Through China*, by Fiona Macdonald, would be a good introductory book to read about this man's life and influence in China. It also introduces them to other key characters and events from that time in history, but the pages are relatively short in text and have many illustrations to hold the young person's interest.

Aztecs and Incas apparently found civilizations in Central and South America within a hundred or so years of each other.

The Hundred Years' War between England and France begins in 1337.

- 📖 For older readers, or for a chapter read-aloud selection for this dynasty, you may consider *The Travels of Marco Polo*, by Marion Koenig, which contains lots of colorful illustrations and memorable events from Marco Polo's experiences. Manuel Komroff's *Marco Polo* biography is also very readable but with minimal illustrations. The Landmark history title by Richard Walsh, *Adventures and Discoveries of Marco Polo*, is actually based on the Marsden translation of Marco Polo's own book. All of these titles make excellent read-aloud choices or are for self-directed readers grades 4 and above.

- ✏ Have students create a collage of information about Marco Polo and his travels as they read and discover what Marco Polo saw, experienced, learned, and accomplished. You may want to have your student initially keep a list of ideas or images that could be used in a collage. Then use pictures cut from magazines, printed off the computer, drawn by hand, etc., to form the collage. Specify a minimum number of images for the collage, which would depend on the age of your child and how much reading you choose to do in this section of history. After the images are artistically arranged, you may want to note on the back of the collage why certain images were used. Your student's mind might have gone off in a different direction than you expected, yet the picture is relevant to the collage when you hear his explanation. For example, he may cut out a picture of white horses and milk. How are those items related to Marco Polo? Well, Polo reported that the Khan owned over 1,000 pure white horses, and members of the Khan's family would drink their milk.

The Black Death comes from Asia to Europe in 1347 and reaches its peak in 1349, killing some 25 million people in Europe alone.

- ✎ Write a story of Marco Polo's adventures from his camel's or horse's perspective. Younger children can dictate their narration to you, while older students can accomplish this creative writing on their own.

- ✎ If you have two children studying this unit at the same time, have them do drama. One child takes on the role of a news reporter for the Italian newspaper *The Venetian Blind*, while the other plays the role of Marco Polo after his return to Venice. Act out this interview for the rest of the family or videotape the interview.

- ♪ One note (well, two eighth notes actually): We noticed there was an opera entitled *Marco Polo* available through our library. Even if you like opera, we would not recommend this very modern (and very bizarre) "musical interpretation" of Polo's life.

Days 5 & 6

Kublai Khan

Use Kublai Khan timeline figure in Appendix C

The Khan was in his fifties when Marco Polo arrived in China. He was ruler over territory that stretched from northern China and Korea, westward through northern India, Afghanistan, Persia, and parts of Russia. The Mongolian empire continued through Armenia, Tibet, and west into Europe, including Hungary and Poland. Kublai Khan had given up the nomadic style of life that he had known as a Mongol warrior and traded it for a life that came to appreciate things of beauty and new ideas more like the Chinese did. He did not quite become "Chinese," however, and even sowed prairie grass in his palace's courtyard to remind him of the Mongolian **steppes** (vast, level, treeless tracts of arid land in southeastern Europe and Asia). Life in the Khan's court was rich and extravagant—walls covered in beaten gold, sidewalks of lapis lazuli, golden serviceware, feasts and festivals, and much more. Hunting parties included hunts of buffalo, bears, and wild boars, but the Khan even used animals such as leopards and tigers in a hunt. The Khan also set up a system of communication throughout his kingdom to link all of his empire. Roads were built from Peking (the capital) throughout the empire, with a posting station located every three miles along the road so that a new messenger could run with the message to the next station. In this manner, a normal ten days' journey could be covered in a 24-hour period. (The Pony Express has nothing on the "Peking Express," so to speak.)

Xanadu

Xanadu was the Khan's summer palace in northern China, on the borders of the land from which the Mongols had originated. It was a palace designed by Chinese architects and made of marble, carved with statues of flowers and animals. Outside the wall of the palace, a 16-mile park was designed; it contained fountains, streams, a deer park for hunting parties, and a bamboo pavilion that could be taken down and set up wherever and whenever the Khan wished.

- and Read Samuel Taylor Coleridge's poem "Kubla Khan," (found in most famous poetry anthologies) and compare it to what you've read about life in the Khan's kingdom. Realize that Coleridge never completed this poem—he awoke from the dream, or "vision," he was having before he completed the poem—so it ends rather abruptly, but it's a unique language arts touch to the whole unit. You could even ask your student to attempt completing the poem for Coleridge.

- Using descriptions provided in various books you may gather about the Kublai Khan, draw a picture of Xanadu.

- Reader's Digest Video and Television designates almost ten minutes to Xanadu in its video *Imperial Splendors*.

It's amazing to think that the China that Marco Polo saw (and believed to be so splendid and magnificent) may have actually been less glorious than what the country was like during the Tang and Song dynasties. The Khan died in 1294, and even though Yuan rulers tried to govern the country kindly, some counselors urged the killing of all Chinese, so Yuan rulers became hated by the Chinese. By the middle of the 14th century, the Mongolian invading machine was winding down, and rebel attacks were beginning to be made.

In 1367, a monk who had become a bandit, named Zhu Yuanzhuang, led a revolt, causing the last Mongol emperor to flee the country. The bandit named himself the new emperor and took on the name of Ming Hong Wu, which was the beginning of the Ming dynasty (1368–1644).

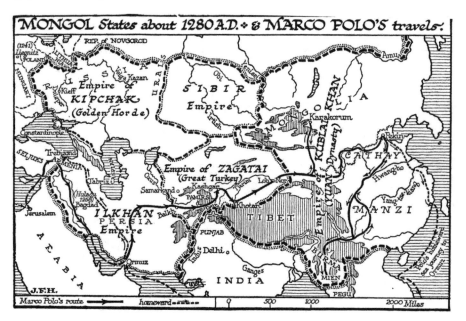

Dynasty #10
The MING Dynasty
A.D. 1368–1644

Recommended Items
- ☐ Sketching supplies (paper and pencil or pen)
- ☐ Video of the Forbidden City (optional)
- ☐ Feldspar sample from a mineral kit

Day 1

Admiral Zheng He

Having driven the Mongols out of the country, the Chinese wanted to return honor and prestige to their people. So they strengthened the Great Wall of China, improved the Grand Canal, built a new capital at Beijing, and sent Admiral Zheng He to visit various foreign rulers. The admiral was first dispatched by Emperor Yong Lo, and between 1405 and 1433, the admiral led seven expeditions into the "Western Ocean" (otherwise known as the Indian Ocean). He commanded a fleet of oceangoing junks from the Chinese navy, some of which were five times the size of the ship that Vasco da Gama used when rounding the Cape of Good Hope 70 years later. The movable **batten sails** and the addition of rudders to steer the junks more easily were tremendous improvements in these naval ships. The admiral commanded approximately 28,000 men on these ships, so it was an enormous convoy. Nevertheless, Zheng He's visits were not of a military or conquest nature; he was simply peacefully demonstrating the naval power of the Chinese.

- Draw a Chinese junk using Lee J. Ames's *Draw 50 Boats, Ships, Trucks and Trains*.

Zheng He's visits to some 30 foreign rulers caused other countries to recognize the Ming dynasty and befriend it. He took gifts to these far-off countries (including Siam, Borneo, Sri Lanka, Persia, Arabia, Africa, and India), and he brought back tributes from the foreign nations. Zheng He's voyages allowed for great amounts of scientific data to be compiled, as well. Unfortunately, in 1479, a jealous government official had Zheng He's records of these journeys destroyed.

Day 2

Forbidden City

The Ming improvements made to the capital of Beijing included the building of the Forbidden City (1406–1420), home of the emperor and his family in the heart of China. For the most part, the city was exclusively for the emperor, who lived in practically total seclusion, guarded by loyal eunuchs. Few Chinese and almost no foreigners were allowed beyond the gates of this special imperial home. A moat and high walls prevented easy entrance into the city, and the gates and terraces all faced south (which, if you will recall, was an important direction in Chinese culture). There were walled gardens, pagodas, lakes, and pavilions in the emperor's exclusive home. It is said that there are 9,999 rooms in the Forbidden City, which means that if a newborn baby lived in one room every day of

John Wycliffe is expelled from Oxford University for opposing Church doctrines.

Constantinople falls to the Ottoman Turks.

Use Forbidden City timeline figure in Appendix C

his life, he would be 27 years old before he had seen the interior of each room! (It makes me grateful that I only have *five* rooms to dust.)

📖 *See Through History: Ancient China*, by Briand Williams, pp. 40, 41, provides an overlay illustration of the finery of the Forbidden City. Zheng Shifeng's *China* and National Geographic Society's *Journey Into China* also have some excellent photos of this imperial palace.

🚐 Travel to China's capital and tour the Forbidden City. It can be written off as an educational expense, right?

🏳 If a live tour is not affordable, try watching Reader's Digest's video *Imperial Splendors*, which has approximately ten minutes of film devoted to the Forbidden City. Almost any travel video of China will probably include shots of the Forbidden City.

Day 3

Ming Vases

One of the most popular forms of porcelain came into existence during the Ming dynasty. The blue and white-pieces associated with Ming porcelain were so famous in the West that they were called "china," named after their point of origin. This new china was exceptionally refined—almost eggshell thin and translucent.

It is said that Ming potters took 72 steps to change the raw clay to porcelain. *Made in China*, p. 43, by Suzanne Williams, explains how, for an entire day, the potters would pound together kaolin clay (fine white clay) from Mt. Kaoliang and another clay called "porcelain stone" (containing feldspar, which creates the chemicals that make porcelain "glass-like"). Then the potters would mix the clay powder in water. The heaviest clay sank. They would pour off the lighter clay—still in the water—and let it dry into an extra fine powder. Enough water to make the powder into a thick paste was then added, which was in turn pressed into molds or shaped on the potter's wheel. The pieces were then dried, polished, and decorated. To make the famous blue and white porcelain, the potters painted designs on the dry pieces with cobalt before they were fired. The pieces were covered with a clear glaze and fired for 24 hours.

🚀 Locate a sample of feldspar in a mineral kit if you have access to one. Have the children do a streak test (to assess its hardness) and a cleavage test (to assess its form) on the feldspar to determine why it would make a good glass-like or strengthening addition to the porcelain process. Any handbook on minerals will aid in this discussion.

It was also during the Ming dynasty that the "Monkey King" became the star of a novel entitled *Journey to the West* by Wu Chengen (written in the 1500s).

"Monkey King"

Monkey's tricks and humor made the Monkey King popular in Chinese culture, similar to legends about King Arthur or tall tales about Paul Bunyan and Pecos Bill. The condensed version of the tale (with a tail) is that Sun Wukong (the Monkey King), who was a "heavenly being," accompanied his master to India searching for the Buddhist religious scriptures, the Tripitaka. Along the journey he endured all kinds of dangers and difficulties, meeting various demons and evil beings, from which he protected his master. His clever,

Vasco da Gama reaches India in 1498.

Martin Luther starts the Reformation with his 95 Theses in 1517.

Sir Walter Raleigh sets up an English colony in Virginia; it fails in 1585.

Ferdinand Magellan sails around Cape Horn in 1520.

cunning, acrobatic, sometimes mischievous character had a good heart, and he was always devoted to the traveling monk. Sun Wukong could change into anything he liked: a bug, a tiger, a gargantuan monkey, etc. He carried a magical club, which he disguised as a needle behind his ear. He could even ride clouds faster than any Chinese god. (Faster than a speeding cloud, more powerful than a tiger, able to step over pagodas in a single bound . . . Look, up in the air! It's "Monkey King"!) The character became perhaps the best-loved character in Chinese operas. There are between 500 and 600 operas around Sun Wukong's adventures and acrobatic antics. The operas are filled with somersaults, tumbles, falls, and spectacular fight scenes.

📖 Ed Young has written a young reader (doubly so, considering the author's last name) entitled *Monkey King*. It is a simplified retelling of the original epic, but it makes no judgment on Buddhist beliefs or gods, so discussion on what is *truth* will definitely need to be included!

Pilgrims land near Cape Cod in 1620.

The "Monkey King"

Dynasty #11
The QING Dynasty or TSING or MANCHU Dynasty
A.D. 1644–1912

Recommended Items

❑   Biography about a missionary (or missionaries) who served in China in the last four centuries.

Day 1

The Ming dynasty came to a close in 1644 when invaders from Manchuria conquered China. The new Manchu, or Qing, dynasty marked the end of imperial China. **Manchurians** were an ethnic group that lived in northeast China, but who were not Chinese. Manchus (or Manchurians) arrived as a barbarian tribe that broke through the Great Wall, and like the Mongols some 600 years before them, the Manchus set up their own dynasty (MacLenighan, *Enchantment of the World: China*, p. 83). These Qing rulers governed China in much the same way the Ming had. Often, Chinese scholars were called upon to serve in civil service and in the emperor's court, which developed Chinese loyalty, in some respects. Kangzi, one of the greatest Qing emperors, even expanded China's control to Taiwan, Mongolia, Tibet, and Xinjiang (Turkistan). The Qing rule appeared strong.

But in other respects, the Qing leaders offended their new minions south of the Great Wall and therein weakened their dynasty. For example, Manchus forced men to shave the fronts of their heads and wear pigtails instead of traditional topknots of hair (MacLenighan, *Enchantment of the World: China*, p. 85). Such a change in hairstyle was a great insult to proud Ming Chinese.

🖌   Color an illustration of Manchurian fashions from Ming-Ju Sun's *Chinese Fashions Coloring Book*.

Qing leadership was also weakened because Manchus feared that other changes in government or trade might lead to Chinese rebellion, so they hung onto outdated traditions. The emperors made it illegal for Chinese ships to sail outside home waters, limited trade with outside nations, and caused Chinese technology to fall behind other countries because they feared that foreign ideas might cause unrest among the Chinese subjects.

The Opium War

Western influence, however, was being felt more and more each year. First, the influence came through trade. British ships brought **opium** from India to trade for China's tea because the Chinese were not interested in Britain's factory goods. The British wanted to sell vast quantities of this drug in China, but the Qing emperors refused its import (for obvious reasons). A clash developed when, in 1839, a Chinese official in Canton tried to stop the British from trading opium in the port. Britain declared war on China and sent gunboats to support the opium traders. They easily defeated the Chinese, forcing China to open four more ports to foreign trade and to give the island of Hong Kong to Britain. This success on Britain's part encouraged other foreign powers (including France, Japan, Russia, and Germany) to influence China, demand trade concessions, and receive territorial awards.

🚀   There is an obvious opportunity to do a research unit or a health unit here on opium and its effects on the body, particularly for older students. At the very

---

Peter the Great of Russia takes complete control of Russia in 1689.

The Glorious Revolution in 1688 sees William of Orange, with a small army of Dutch soldiers, delivering England from Catholicism.

The French-Indian War and the American Revolution introduce British battles to North American soil.

The French Revolution begins in 1789.

Napoleon invades Russia in 1812.

America's Civil War staggers the nation from 1861–1865, and beyond.

The Boer War in Africa (also known as the South African War) begins in 1880, creating conflict between the Boers and the British.

least, one should mention that even a lovely flower, such as a poppy, can be used for sinful purposes when man warps what God meant for beauty and good. *Focus on Opiates*, by Susan DeStafano, explains to fifth and sixth graders how opiates can be used for healing or for harm. Portions of Chapters 3 and 4 (up to page 40) are really the only sections I would recommend because they focus on the scientific and biological effects that opiates have on the brain. The rest of the book seems to make excuses for an addict's sin.

Days 2 & 3

Rebellions Arise

From 1851–1864, a civil war called the Taiping Rebellion took the lives of millions of Chinese. By 1900, an antiforeign society called the Boxers destroyed imported goods and attacked Christian missionaries. Boxers were a spin-off of a secret society called "The White Lotus." The Boxers were a fierce sect of marital arts adherents who wielded their anger and violence against white, evil Westerners (the "invaders"), rather than against the Empress Dowager, whose extravagance was actually causing many of the nation's problems. This uprising was known as the Boxer Rebellion, but it was unsuccessful in reclaiming Chinese control because the superior firepower of the international forces suppressed the rebellion and occupied Beijing.

 📖 Read a biography about any of a number of missionaries who influenced China. Many of these missionaries were willing to sacrifice their very lives to share the truth of the Gospel with the people of China. James Hudson Taylor, James O. Fraser, Gladys Aylward, Grace Service, Eric Liddell, John and Betty Stam, Isobel Kuhn, and even Ruth Bell Graham are options for this reading activity. (The Stams fit perfectly within the time frame of the Boxer Rebellion.) Then have your student give an oral book report on this biography.

Finally, by 1911, Sun Yat-sen, leader of the Kuomintang (National People's Party), led the Chinese to overthrow the weakened Manchu rulers and to establish a republic. The last Qing emperor, Puyi, was forced to step down in 1912, ending nearly 5,000 years of dynastic rule!

 📖 Pearl Buck wrote a book entitled *The Man Who Changed China* for the Landmark series. Sun Yat-sen is considered the "Father of Modern China" because he worked for a government of, by, and for the people until his death in 1925. While Buck's book is well written stylistically, I'll be honest and say that I think its content aggrandizes Sun Yat-sen in many ways. His own family life testifies that he was not the saint that Buck tends to emphasize. Nevertheless, Sun Yat-sen's charisma and the dynamics of the revolution that he encouraged in China are clearly presented.

Day 4

Puyi—The Last Emperor

Exploration Into China (Tao, pp. 38, 39) gives a more detailed history of Puyi's sad story. The evil Empress Dowager (Ci Xi) had chosen 2-year-old Puyi as emperor after she had imprisoned her own husband. Since Puyi was not old enough to rule, the

Cuba is freed during the Spanish-American War in 1898. (Teddy Roosevelt's Rough Riders become heroes.)

Rumblings of the first of two world wars in the 20th century begin to be heard by 1912.

Empress Dowager had intended to control the government. She died only months later, leaving an infant as emperor. When Puyi was 5, China became a **republic** (a country with an elected government rather than one ruled by a monarch or king/queen). Puyi was allowed to continue living in the Forbidden City with his attendants, but relations with the new government kept deteriorating. He was forced to flee to a Japanese colony in 1924. When Japan invaded Manchuria in 1931, Puyi was made emperor of the Japanese "puppet state," meaning he had no real authority, but he was given the title of "emperor" of that region. Hatred toward this former emperor arose, however, and when the Russian army arrested him after World War II, he was required to spend time in a Chinese prison until 1959. He spent the remainder of his life working as a gardener in Peking, where he died in 1967.

📺 *The Last Emperor* video fits perfectly in this time frame of study, but we have reservations (to say the least) about recommending it for use in this unit. *The Last Emperor* presents Hollywood's version of this tragic final emperor and the conclusion of the Chinese dynasties, but it's exactly that—*Hollywood's* version. Thankfully, my husband and I previewed this video before introducing it to our children. We only watched about 15 minutes of the film and we began feeling squeamish, so we shut it off (and left it off). It does provide a full-color view of what life in the Forbidden City and as the emperor may have been like, but there were elements of the story within those first few minutes that already caused us to question the value of the film for our family. It will have to be your choice, but I would highly encourage you as a parent to view it before your children (even your older children) see it to make certain you are prepared to explain and discuss many of the scenes.

The Boxer Rebellion

Chapter 5
The MODERN *Period*
1912 to Present

Post-Dynastic China

Recommended Items

❑   Coloring page of Communist China flag from Appendix C
❑   Voice of the Martyrs newsletter or website access

Day 1

After Puyi's abdication of the imperial throne, a 20-year-long conflict developed. Nationalists ruled China from 1928–1949 and tried to establish a **democracy** in China, a government by the people, following the rule of the majority. Communists began asserting their influence during this time, and the result was internal war. **Communism** is an economic system and a humanistic form of government in which all means of production—including land, natural resources, even families—are used by the government supposedly for the "good" of all its members. Basically, another civil war ensued in the early 1930s, with the new leader of the Nationalists, Chiang Kai-shek, obsessed with destroying the Communists.

📖   Ferroa's *Cultures of the World: China,* pp. 26–29, supplies a more in-depth explanation of modern China's upheaval and unrest.

The Long March and Communism's Influence

The Long March in 1934 was a move by the Communist Red Army to avoid the Nationalists by climbing over 18 mountain ranges, crossing 24 rivers, and trekking some 6,000 miles on foot so that Yan'an could become their headquarters. Only one in five of those who began the march lived through it. A former teacher, Mao Zedong (or Mao Tse-tung), led this march and became one of the founding members of the Chinese Communist Party. In Yan'an they conducted guerrilla warfare and educational programs (Chinese Communism's roots). The Chinese were so involved with their own conflict, however, that they ignored the threatening movements of Japanese troops, which had entered China in the 1930s. The Sino-Japanese War began in 1937, adding to the internal destruction and conflict that China was already experiencing. As conditions worsened, the people of China became united in their effort to rid their nation of Japanese control. The Japanese remained in eastern China until World War II, but upon Japan's defeat by America, China was freed from Japanese influence in 1945. The internal struggle for power continued until the Nationalists moved to the island of Taiwan when the Communist Party took over the country in 1949.

Days 2 & 3

📖   Meindert DeJong's *The House of Sixty Fathers* deals with a young Chinese boy escaping the invading Japanese army. It's a good read-aloud choice, or it is appropriate for grades 4 and above reading alone.

Use Mao Zedong timeline figure in Appendix C

51

Chapter 6
Unit Wrap-Up

There you have it; that brings us to current times in the history of China. You've covered over 5,000 years in approximately 12 weeks. (Warp-Speed Time Travel, at your service!)

Day 1

⧗ Have students compile their copybook work, art projects, writing activities, and so forth in correct chronological order as a portfolio of their work for this unit study. (This is a great way to review the material studied at the same time.)

Day 2

✂ Grades K-3: Complete the crossword puzzle in Appendix B as a means of reviewing this study on China.

♀ Grades 4-6: Complete the reproducible quiz on China (in Appendix B) to review material covered in this unit study and to evaluate recall of major facts.

Day 3

✂ Now have a final "Chinese festival" at which each student displays art projects, copybooks, science experiments, and such for a parent or grandparents who may not have been able to participate actively in the unit study. Students could even demonstrate papermaking, act out the Marco Polo interview, or quote Samuel T. Coleridge's "Kubla Khan." Essentially, it gives your children a chance to review the past 12 weeks of study. Conclude the evening by praying for the people of China who need to hear of a Savior Who loved them so much that He died on the cross for their sins. And pray for believers in China who are suffering daily for the sake of Christ.

No Regrets

A Chinese proverb states, "Flowers leave some of their fragrance in the hand that bestows them." I know that in studying for this unit, I have discovered information about China and its history that I never would have learned otherwise. I'm thankful for the "fragrance" of Cathay that was left on my educational hands as I bestowed these lessons on my children.

Of even greater importance, my children have obtained an entire bouquet of knowledge about China! They will remember the significance of dragons in China because of our reading and copybook work. They are familiar with dynasty names because of our ongoing timeline and can recall terra-cotta soldiers and the effects of dam construction because of our hands-on activities. They recognize oriental music by its five tones because of their exposure to Chinese culture, and they have mental hooks for hanging more information about Qin Shih Huang-Ti, Mongols, the Forbidden City, silk, and porcelain as they encounter these topics in later studies. They are praying more heartily for believers in China because they have learned that Chinese Christians face daily persecution. Most importantly, we all have a greater appreciation for the Sovereign God we serve, Who is orchestrating all of these events, and Who *allows* individuals like Marco Polo, Confucius, James Hudson Taylor, and Gladys Aylward to affect all of earth's history.

Unit studies may not be the least time-consuming approach to education. However, if the education we give to our families can be God-centered, delightful, multisensory, intriguing, thought provoking, and memorable, I'm not sure what more we could want! You will *never* regret your labors in unit studies, and your children will thank you for avoiding the "drone zone" in history study.

Appendix A
Grades 7–12 Supplement

General Suggestions

Preteens and teens can assist in finding resources in the library at the unit's start, in reading or skimming for material within those resources that relates to a given subtopic, and even in reading along with or aloud to younger students/siblings. We learn best when we *teach* a topic, so why not have your 7th to 12th graders do deeper reading and research on a given subtopic and then present that material to the rest of the family in an oral report or in a lesson of their own creation? It gives the students practice in public speaking, forces them to explain concepts clearly, and causes them to work with the data three times (reading, formulating lessons, and presenting) versus only once (reading).

Older students can (and *should*) be required to do more writing with their unit studies—in terms of both copybook work and other research projects or writing assignments. Copybook material can be simple facts about things studied during each day—little-known tidbits or interesting information that captivates your teen—or it can be a chronological text of data about the unit being studied. Research projects can delve deeper into subtopics presented to your younger students in a unit, or they can focus on an area of interest related to the unit. (In this unit on China, for instance, a student could further research the history of the island of Hong Kong and its political release from British control to Chinese sovereignty in 1997.)

The research ideas and critical thinking suggestions already given within this study lend themselves to writing assignments for your junior high and high school students. Make certain they truly ponder their approach, writing style, mechanics, and content before they turn in an assignment. Remind them that writing is a process and that polishing an assignment requires time and effort on their part. The ultimate goal is to express ideas, information, and opinions clearly—to God's glory.

Because older students can reason and develop ideas at a deeper level than our K–6 students, we should challenge them with these critical thinking and research questions. Have them deal with comparison-contrast issues—both within the topic (as already provided in the K–6 unit study) and related to other topics or current issues. (For example, teens could compare and contrast Chairman Mao Zedong's form of communism in China with Fidel Castro's form in Cuba.)

Don't forget to use a variety of media, resources, senses, and assignments to maintain your teens' interest and to increase recall of the studied material. Older students appreciate variety as much as (perhaps even more than) younger students. Allow your teens to explore and examine those issues or ideas that intrigue them the most. The quality of work you receive from your students, as well as their retention of the material, will directly coincide with their interest and involvement with a topic. If they initiate a project or attack a book of their own volition, more power to them! What we may see as a "rabbit trail" in the unit has the potential to lead your teens to an unrivaled "garden" of food for thought or beauty in discovery.

Specific Suggestions

In addition to the activities, questions, and projects already proposed in the K–6 unit (including the timeline and copybook information), additional specific assignments for individual research and work could be given to your 7–12 students. We have written these specific suggestions directly *to* older students, hoping to encourage independent work on their part. As parents, however, you can help each of your teen-age students determine which and how many projects within each section or dynasty he (or she) should attempt in the time you have for this Chinese unit study. Then, establish a deadline or independent work contract with the teen so that he fulfills his assignment(s) in a timely manner.

Geography Lessons

- Choose one of the five autonomous regions of China for further research, and then give a five-minute oral presentation on its unique geographic features. You can even play the role of a tour guide taking tourists through this region on their trip, "visiting" points of interest along the way.

- Sketch or paint one of the animals indigenous to China.

- Imagine you are a fisherman on the Yangtze River. Write a diary or journal entry on how a typical day of fishing changed drastically because of the new Three Gorges Dam project. (This may require some research as well as creativity.)

- Prepare an entire Chinese meal, complete with Chinese character menus and chopsticks.

- Research Chinese names and choose one that you feel describes your personality or describes virtues that you would like to demonstrate. Be prepared to explain your findings and name choice to your parent or family.

- Plan a trip to China, including methods of travel, places/attractions to visit, and budgeting needs for your family. (Web sites, travel offices, travel books, and other resources can be used in this project.)

- Design a travel poster inviting tourists to China.

History Lessons

The Hsia Dynasty

- and Write and illustrate a children's book about the landing of Noah's Ark on Mt. Ararat and then the dispersal of the nations from Shem, Ham, and Japheth to various regions of the world.

- Present an argument paper on why Peking man is such a questionable archaeological "proof" of evolution. (See Gabriel Arquilevich's *Fairview's Guide to Composition and Essay Writing*, or Patrick Sebranek's *Writer's Inc.* for more on argument essays.)

- Imagine you are a reporter for a newspaper in 1939, and your editor selects you to write an article on the original discovery of Peking Man's bone and its recent disappearance. Remember to provide answers to the 5 "W" questions (who, what, when, where, and why) in the opening paragraph of the article, as a professional newspaper reporter should.

The Shang Dynasty

Write a comparative essay on the ambiguity and falsehoods that any form of divination contains (whether in horoscopes, tarot cards, oracle bones, or psychic readings). Recall that all of these forms of divination go against God's sovereignty. Include biblical proof of God's control over life and scriptural warnings about divination. (See *Jensen's Format Writing,* by Frode Jensen, or Patrick Sebranek's *Writer's Inc.* for more information on comparison essays.)

Research how bronze is actually produced. Perhaps you could even visit the studio of an artist who uses bronze for sculpting or go to a store that bronzes baby shoes and such.

Compare the price of sewing a dress in cotton cloth versus silk. Also identify why silk is a preferred fabric for certain items or garments. (Why was silk often selected for parachutes, for example?)

Get some hemp rope and unravel it; then attempt to weave it into cloth. Make a coaster or a placemat out of the hemp. (We don't recommend hemp t-shirts or sweaters, purely for comfort's sake.)

The Zhou Dynasty

Create a poster showing the hierarchy of control in the Chinese feudal system; illustrate it with pictures appropriate for each class and informative captions if desired.

Write a comparison and contrast paper on Confucianism and Taoism. (Again, see *Jensen's Format Writing* or *Writer's Inc.* for more explanation on this style of essay.) Or write an imagined conversation among Confucius, Lao Tzu, and Jesus Christ in which Christ explains the *True* Way as the others present their philosophies.

Develop a scavenger hunt for another member of your house using a needle compass (as explained in the K–6 unit) to provide directions.

The Tsin Dynasty

Determine whether the Chinese have other names for constellations already recognized in the Northern Hemisphere and what the stories behind those other names may be. Give an oral report—including visual aids of the constellations—to your family.

Map the extent of territory captured by the Huns throughout Asia and Europe.

Imagine that you are one of the sculptors of the terra-cotta army. Write a letter to a family member describing your job (difficulties you're facing, artistic touches you are including, reasons for creating the soldiers, etc.).

Draw or embroider a dragon resembling those used to symbolize the First Emperor.

Research other mythical creatures that are sometimes used in Chinese art—such as unicorns, Fo dogs, feng-huangs, and celestial toads. Provide an illustration of each creature and a brief explanation of its symbolism in Chinese art.

The Han Dynasty

and Visit a local music store or a Chinese store and see if you can experiment with an original Chinese instrument. Or look for an upcoming concert in your area featuring a Chinese instrumentalist, and enjoy an evening of music appreciation in five tones.

and Attend *The Nutcracker* ballet (which includes "The Chinese Dance" in it) and write a review of the production for a newspaper. (You may need to read some theatrical reviews in your local paper to follow the review style used.) Emphasize the accuracy or beauty of "The Chinese Dance" within your review.

Research seismographs, Richter scales, and earthquakes. Explain how seismographs work today, and compare them with the ones from the Han dynasty.

Read Ravi Zacharias's *The Lotus and the Cross: Jesus Talks with Buddha*.

Compose a short tract that biblically refutes the concept of reincarnation and then presents the message of salvation and eternal life through Jesus Christ.

The Sui Dynasty

Draw cartoon illustrations of how flash-locks and pound-locks on a canal from the Sui dynasty worked. You can also draw an illustration of how locks on a more modern canal work. This assignment, obviously, may require some research.

The Tang Dynasty

Write 8 to 12 lines of poetry that imitate the Chinese intent of capturing emotions as expressed in natural phenomena.

Write an interpretation of a Chinese poem that you particularly like. What does the poem *mean*? What theme is dominant throughout the poem? What images, colors, sounds, and even word lengths are used to help convey the given emotions?

Take a pottery class, or visit a pottery studio and observe the artist in action.

Design your own Chinese papercut, seeing how detailed you can possibly make it.

Research and list the periodic table symbols and chemical amounts required for each element to formulate gunpowder. You could also research where saltpeter is collected, or find your own sample of saltpeter.

The Song Dynasty

- Take a watercolors painting class, or watch a video course on this art form, and then attempt your own visual interpretation of your poem from the Tang dynasty.

- Use calligraphy pens or calligraphic painting to rewrite your Tang poem; then mount it in a frame with your watercolor painting from above.

- Read more about armillary spheres, and write a brief summary of their importance in science (particularly astronomy and navigation).

- Research acupuncture or moxibustion more thoroughly, and then write an opinion paper on whether or not a Christian should use these forms of medical treatment.

- Read all of Harold Lamb's *Genghis Khan and the Mongol Horde* or *Genghis Khan: The Emperor of All Men* and present a dramatic monologue (for your family) of his life or of a key experience in his life.

The Yuan Dynasty

- Read Marsden's translation of Marco Polo's original book, *The Travels of Marco Polo, the Venetian.*

- Plan a screenplay proposal for a film about Marco Polo. Include information such as whom you would choose to play the various characters in the tale, what specific incidents would be included in the film, and how you would introduce and conclude the film in such a way that best captures your audience's attention.

- Write a traditional play or a puppet play of the possible dialogue between Genghis Khan and Kublai Khan in which the topic of conversation focuses on Genghis Khan's reaction to Kublai's summer palace, Xanadu. Genghis Khan never saw his heir's extravagant palace, so this is all an utterly imaginary conversation. You can make it a comedy or a drama, but then present the play to your family.

- Memorize Samuel Coleridge's "Kubla Khan." Read an interpretation of the poem in a book of poetry and determine whether you agree or disagree with the proffered interpretation.

The Ming Dynasty

- and Research more on Admiral Zheng He's life and travels as a Chinese goodwill ambassador. Write a magazine article about this great traveler for *Time* or *World* magazine as you would expect it to have appeared in the 1400s.

- and Study more about the Forbidden City. Write a real estate summary of this piece of property as though it were up for sale to the average citizen. Highlight its unique features, dimensions, number of rooms, etc. (Have some fun with this assignment!)

- Draw your own illustrations of the Monkey King, based on reading *Monkey King* (Ed Young's young-reader story of this legendary character's life), or on any other research you've done on this character from Chinese lore.
- Check your library's foreign films selection to see if any Chinese operas are available. View this foreign film, noticing how acrobatics and elaborate masks are mainstays in Chinese opera.

The Qing Dynasty

- Research what forms of treatment are used to help opium addicts be "released" or rehabilitated from their addiction and the success rates of these different forms of treatment. Write an opinion paper on why you believe one form of addiction treatment is better than any other method.
- Write an argument essay on whether or not an addiction is a *disease,* and therefore, whether or not treatment/drug rehabilitation should be covered by insurance companies. You must have statistical or biblical support for your position.
- and ⚰ Read a missionary biography of someone who served in China, and create a collage representing that missionary's life and ministry. Use these pictures, illustrations, maps, and so forth to summarize his or her service for Christ. Be prepared to explain the elements of your collage to your parents or siblings. A listing of missionaries to consider is provided in the K-6 text.
- Read more on the life of Puyi, the last emperor of China. Imagine you are a biographical author who is allowed to interview Puyi about his experiences in changing China. List 20 specific questions you would like to ask him. (You could even write these questions *before* reading any more about his life, and then see if you can write responses to the questions as you discover answers within your reading and research.)

The Modern Period

- Read a biography of Mao Zedong, and attempt to write a summary of his Communist vision or plan for China.
- Watch a video of the Tiananmen Square demonstrations and discuss with your parents why you believe those uprisings developed. (For example, were they the result of frustration with Communism, or were they merely "Generation X" urges to revolt?)
- Establish a pen-pal relationship with someone in China or with one of your church's missionaries to China.
- and ✏ Read *Chinese Cinderella*, by Adeline Yen Mah, and *Red Scarf Girl* by Ji-li Jiang. Write a book review comparing and contrasting the two stories, and then rate each one on a scale of one to five stars for enjoyment, readability, and educational value.

Unit Wrap-Up

♀ Create a review test of this unit on China, including a variety of types of questions (multiple-choice, true/false, matching, short answer, essay, etc.). Be sure to determine the age for which this test is intended, and ask questions appropriate for that age/grade. You will also need to supply an answer key.

✏ and ✂ In addition to all copybook work and hands-on projects completed during this unit on the Orient, collect all your essays and research papers for this unit into one portfolio or notebook. It will serve as an excellent compilation of writing samples, as well as providing a great unit review resource.

Older students (grades 4-6) should be able to complete this quiz on their own. Younger students (grades K-3) may complete it with parental assistance, listening to the questions read aloud and then dictating answers to the teacher.

For true/false questions, please circle the correct letter: T for true, if you agree with the statement; F for false, if you disagree with the statement.

For multiple choice questions, please circle the letter of the answer that *best* completes the sentence or answers the question.

For fill-in-the blank questions, supply the missing word(s) to complete the statement or answer the question.

For short answer questions, please provide the information requested—being certain to give the requested number of answers or items.

China Quiz

1. On which continent does China rest? _____

2. T   or   F   China is entirely south of the equator.

3. Name three physical features (mountain ranges, rivers, cities, etc.) that are unique to China.

4. China experiences heavy rainfalls along its east coast and the Tropic of Cancer. Much of this rainfall comes as the result of the periodic wind system that draws up moist air from the Indian Ocean. What is this wind system called that can bring 60 to 80 inches of rain in China each year? _____.

5. Why are the Yellow and Yangtze rivers key to China? (Supply *one* answer; there are several possible answers.)
    _____

6. Boats unique to China on its waterways are called:
    a. kowtows and jades   c. junks and tangrams
    b. cormorants and paddies   d. junks and sampans

7. What is a staple food grown in paddies of water in China? _____

8. Name one Biblical character who is believed to have established China around 2240 B.C.
    _____

9. The Chinese written language uses a stylized picture or symbol to represent a word. This picture is known as a _____.

10. During the Shang dynasty, metalworkers created an alloy of copper and tin to make spears, cooking pots, and other tools. What is this metal mixture called?

_____

11. What insect's cocoon was discovered to be useful for weaving fine cloth? (Hint: The cloth is called the same thing as the first part of this insect's name.)

12. What is one thing that was unique (sadly enough) about a Shang king's burial? (If you did not study this portion of the unit, skip on to the next question.)

13. T or F   During the Zhou dynasty, a man named Buddha began promoting a philosophy based on kindness, respect, sympathy, and courage. This philosophy became known as Confucianism.

14. Chinese alchemists in the Zhou dynasty noticed that lodestones all contained an iron ore called magnetite, and that flowing lodestones always point the same direction. From these floating lodestones the Chinese invented:
    a. bronze halberds   c. mirrors
    b. compasses   d. crossbow arrowheads

15. T or F   An abacus is a hand-operated calculating machine.

16. Qin Shih Huang-Ti, the First Emperor of the Tsin dynasty, promoted several significant building projects. Can you name *one* of them? (Hint: One project was enormously long, and one project was militarily creative.)_____

17. Do you remember what symbol the First Emperor selected for his clothing and jewelry decorations to represent his wisdom, strength, and life-giving power?

_____.

18. After the Tsin dynasty, the largest ethnic group in China took control of the country (228 B.C.). What was the name of that dynasty, which still remains the largest ethnic group in the world with over one billion people? (Hint: It was named after its emperor Han Gaozu.)

_____

19. During the same dynasty, a new type of bow was made that could be pulled tighter, shot farther, and aimed better than regular bows. It was called the _____.

20. Also in the Han dynasty, cumbersome bamboo books were replaced by what kind of books—something we take for granted now?_____

21. During the Sui dynasty, the spread of Buddhism from India was more evident because of Far Eastern towers that are still used as Buddhist libraries or places of worship. Such towers (usually with curved roofs at each story) are called:
    a. pagodas
    b. nirvanas
    c. yin and yangs
    d. jades

22. Emperor Yang Di, of the Sui dynasty, proposed a project that connected the Yellow, Yangtze, Huai, and Qiantang rivers, and linked the then capital of Loyang with Beijing. This waterway is known as the _____.

23. Works of beauty were praised and encouraged in the Tang dynasty. Can you name *two* types of art work that were promoted in the Tang dynasty? (Several possible answers are available to use.) _____ and _____

24. What mixture of charcoal, sulfur, and saltpeter (which explodes when heated) was invented during the Tang dynasty?_____

25. During the Song dynasty there were three forms of artistic expression that were considered the greatest accomplishments in the arts. They were called the "Three Perfections" and were made up of:
    a.   music, poetry, and fireworks
    b.   papercuts, painting, and sketching
    c.   painting, poetry, and calligraphy
    d.   pagodas, poetry, and music

26. The Chinese zodiac moves in a cycle of 12 years, assigning a different symbol with each year. What symbols are used in the Chinese zodiac? (If you did not study this subtopic of the China unit, please skip this question.)
    a. flowers
    b. animals
    c. kite designs
    d. foods

27. Toward the end of the Song dynasty an invasion of Mongol hordes from the north was led by Temujin, who became better known by his name which means "Emperor of All Men." His new name was
    a. Genghis Khan
    b. Lao Tzu
    c. Marco Polo
    d. Kublai Khan

28. What is a yurt to the Mongols?

29. The Yuan dynasty was led by Genghis Khan's heir, Kublai Khan. One of Kublai Khan's foreign advisors was a young man from Italy. His name was _____ _____, a name that is also used in a totally unrelated vocal water game often played in the swimming pool.

30.   T or F The Silk Road and the Spice Route are different names for the same road connecting China with Rome.

31.   T or F The people of Italy initially did not believe the Polos about the glories of China and the Khan's wealth until they revealed the jewels hidden in the linings of their garments.

32.   Can you briefly explain what Xanadu was to the Kublai Khan?

33.   In the Ming dynasty, Admiral Zheng He was sent out on seven expeditions into the Indian Ocean with a fleet of oceangoing junks from the Chinese navy in order to:
    a.   conquer all lands and peoples he encountered.
    b.   explore unknown waters to the west.
    c.   demonstrate China's naval power and help other countries befriend the Ming dynasty.
    d.   haul away the numerous loads of garbage from China's shore.
    e.   test the new movable batten sails on the junks.

34.   A special home for the emperor and his family was built in the heart of Beijing during the Ming dynasty. Most Chinese and almost all foreigners were forbidden from entering this special city, so it became known as the _____
    _____.

35.   One of the most popular forms of porcelain in China came into existence during the Ming dynasty. These blue and white pieces associated with Ming porcelain simply came known as
    _____.

36.   The Qing dynasty overthrew the Ming rulers when this group invaded China from the north in 1644:
    a. Manchurians   c. Mandolins
    b. Mongols   d. Marco Polos

37.   The name of the last Chinese emperor, who stepped down in 1912, ending nearly 5,000 years of dynastic rule was
    a. Mao Zedong   c. Kublai Khan
    b. Sun Yat-sen   d. Puyi

38.   What political party (led by Mao Zedong or Chairman Mao) took control of China's government in 1949, and has remained the party in power since then? The
    _____ Party.

39.   Name two hardships or difficulties a person living in China today must endure.

40.   What was your favorite project, person, or event that we covered in this unit study of ancient China?

Ancient China Puzzle

Across

1. A series of rulers from the same line of descent, or a powerful group that maintains its position for a considerable amount of time.
3. The Italian trader who lived in China and served as an advisor for the Kublai Khan for over 20 years.
5. Porcelain vases that are blue and white in coloring, and almost eggshell thin, come from this dynasty. It is also the dynasty during which the Forbidden City was built.
6. What useful navigational tool can be formed from a magnetized ore called magnetite or lodestone?
12. The leader who began invading China from the north in 1190 with his "Mongol hordes," and then named himself "Emperor of All Men."
14. A weapon that shoots straighter and farther than a regular bow, but has a triggering system for releasing the bowstring.
15. The symbol associated with the First Emperor, which represented wisdom, strength, helpfulness. We think of it as monstrous, but the Chinese picture it as life-giving and kind (whether it is fire-breathing or not).
17. The staple food of China that is grown in paddies of water.
18. Chinese ships with quilted sails that have absolutely nothing to do with garbage, even though their name may seem like it.
19. Another word for a Chinese written character, or the picture or symbol that represents a word.

Down

2. It is possible that this famous Biblical character and his son, Shem, actually started the first Chinese dynasty along the Yellow River.
4. Porcelain made in China became so refined that it was almost eggshell thin and translucent, so it became known as

_____.

7. The fine cloth woven from the strands of the cocoon of a silkworm.
8. The explosive mixture of charcoal, sulfur, and saltpeter.
9. The wind system that causes wet and dry weather in India and southern Asia, and is usually associated with heavy rain and winds.
10. Huang-Ti, the First Emperor of China, constructed an elaborate tomb for himself, guarded by 6,000 soldiers and horses made of this special clay.
11. A 2,500 mile road that linked the Han and the Roman empires, and allowed trade between Beijing and Rome.

Choose your answers from the following options:

China
Compass
Cross Bow
Dragon
Dynasty
Genghis Khan
Grand Canal
Great Wall
Gun Powder

Junks
Marco Polo
Ming
Monsoon
Noah
Pictogram
Rice
Silk
Silk Road
Terra Cotta

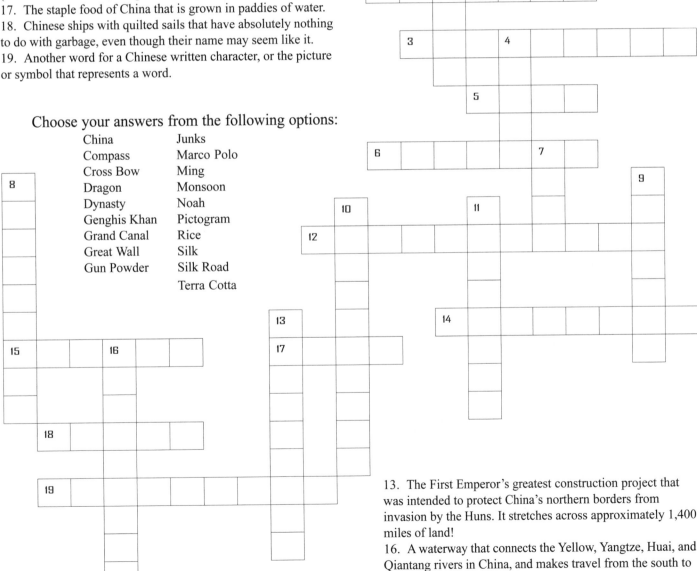

13. The First Emperor's greatest construction project that was intended to protect China's northern borders from invasion by the Huns. It stretches across approximately 1,400 miles of land!
16. A waterway that connects the Yellow, Yangtze, Huai, and Qiantang rivers in China, and makes travel from the south to the north much safer during the Sui dynasty.

China Quiz Answer Key

1. Asia
2. False
3. Answers will vary, but can include the Himalayas; Yellow, Yangtze, and Pearl rivers; Hong Kong; Macao; Taiwan; Beijing; Canton; Hainan Island; Gobi Desert; the Great Wall; the Grand Canal; Manchuria; Shanghai; Turpan Depression, etc.
4. Monsoon
5. Answers will vary: Travel, transportation, hydroelectric power, and irrigation.
6. d.   junks and sampans
7. Rice
8. Noah or Shem
9. Pictogram or character
10. Bronze
11. Silkworm
12. Captives, servants, animals, and other living possessions of the king were killed and buried with the Shang king.
13. False
14. b.   compasses
15. True
16. The Great Wall or the Terra-Cotta Army
17. Dragon
18. Han
19. Crossbow
20. Paper
21. a.   pagodas
22. The Grand Canal
23. Answers will vary and can include porcelain, lacquerware, Chinese paper lanterns, and papercuts.
24. Gunpowder
25. c.   painting, poetry, and calligraphy
26. b.   animals
27. a.   Genghis Khan
28. A yurt is a tent-like domed dwelling.
29. Marco Polo
30. False
31. True
32. Xanadu was his summer palace in northern China where he hunted, enjoyed lovely gardens, and avoided the heat of Peking in the summer.
33. c.   demonstrate China's naval power and help other countries befriend the Ming dynasty.
34. Forbidden City
35. China
36. a.   Manchurians
37. d.   Puyi
38. Communist

39. Answers will vary, but could include such ideas as: religious freedoms are highly limited, family size is regulated by the government, government is not truly democratic, outspoken political dissenters are in danger for their lives, people of education or wealth are denounced, etc.

40. Answers will vary, and we hope they do!

Answers to the Ancient China Puzzle

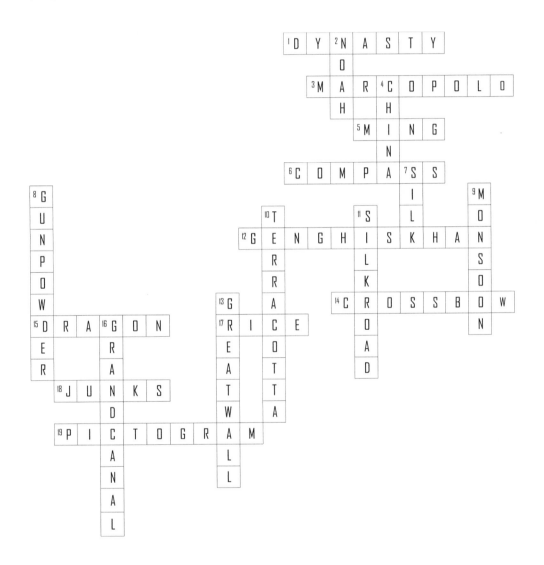

Appendix C
Timeline Figures, China's Flag & Maps

Noah
2948 B.C.–1998 B.C.
Noah, known as Yao in China, is believed to have ruled as emperor in China from 2240 to 1998 B.C. He is believed to have established civilization along the Yellow River after the Great Flood of 2348–2347 B.C.

Lao Tzu
6ᵗʰ century B.C.
A Chinese philosopher who is often pictured riding a water buffalo because of his belief that all living things must live in harmony with nature in order to be wise and happy. His philosophies became known as Taoism

Buddha
563?–483 B.C.
An Indian philosopher whose name means "Enlightened One," and whose ideas and writings became the religion of Buddhism. Buddhism spread to China during the Han dynasty (228 B.C.–A.D. 220). It supposedly reveals the way of salvation from suffering (called a state of Nirvana) by denying oneself worldly desires.

Genghis Khan
1167–1227
Originally known as Temujin, he united the nomadic Mongolian tribes to attack northern China, and took the name Genghis Khan, meaning "Emperor of All Men." He and his Mongol hordes captured northern China and India, Korea, Afghanistan, Persia, and portions of Russia.

Confucius
551?–479? B.C.
A Far Eastern philosopher and teacher who believed that all people are born good and should help one another. His principles for good government and personal behavior became known as the philosophy of Confucianism.

Qin Shih Huang-Ti
259–210 B.C.
This leader of the Qin state conquered other warring states and established himself as the "First Emperor" of a unified China in 221 B.C. He organized construction of the Great Wall of China to protect the northern border of China, and an army of 6,000 terra cotta soldiers to guard his tomb.

Great Wall of China
3ʳᵈ century B.C.– A.D. 16ᵗʰ century
A wall built to protect China's northern border. It is made of stone and earthen fortifications that stretch approximately 1,400 miles. It is sometimes called "the longest cemetery in the world" because so many peasants died in its construction.

Kublai Khan
1215–1294
A descendant of Genghis Khan who extended the Mongol empire from the Pacific Ocean to the Black Sea. He also founded the Yuan dynasty (1279–1368) in China, and was the ruler during Marco Polo's visit.

China's flag has a red field with golden-yellow stars.

Marco Polo
1254–1324
A traveler from Venice who visited Asia on the Silk Road and became Kublai Khan's advisor. He stayed in Asia over 20 years, recording his numerous experiences and observations. These notes later were transcribed into a book, Travels of Marco Polo, the Venetian, *a book that inspired other explorers like Christopher Columbus.*

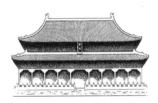

Forbidden City
1406–1420
Built by the Ming dynasty in the heart of the capital of Beijing, the Forbidden City was the exclusive home of the emperor and his family. The emperor was practically in total seclusion, guarded by eunuchs, and moat, and high walls.

Mao Zedong
1893–1976
Also known as Chairman Mao, he was the founder of the People's Republic of China and the Chinese Communist Party. He became, essentially, the law in China—challenging and destroying traditional Chinese culture and laws. His Cultural Revolution program damaged education, economics, and religious freedom, but it did not end class struggle and population "overgrowth."

Three Gorges Dam
21st Century
A controversial hydroelectric dam project underway on the Yangtze River. It is believed it will be the largest structure ever built when it is completed in 2009.

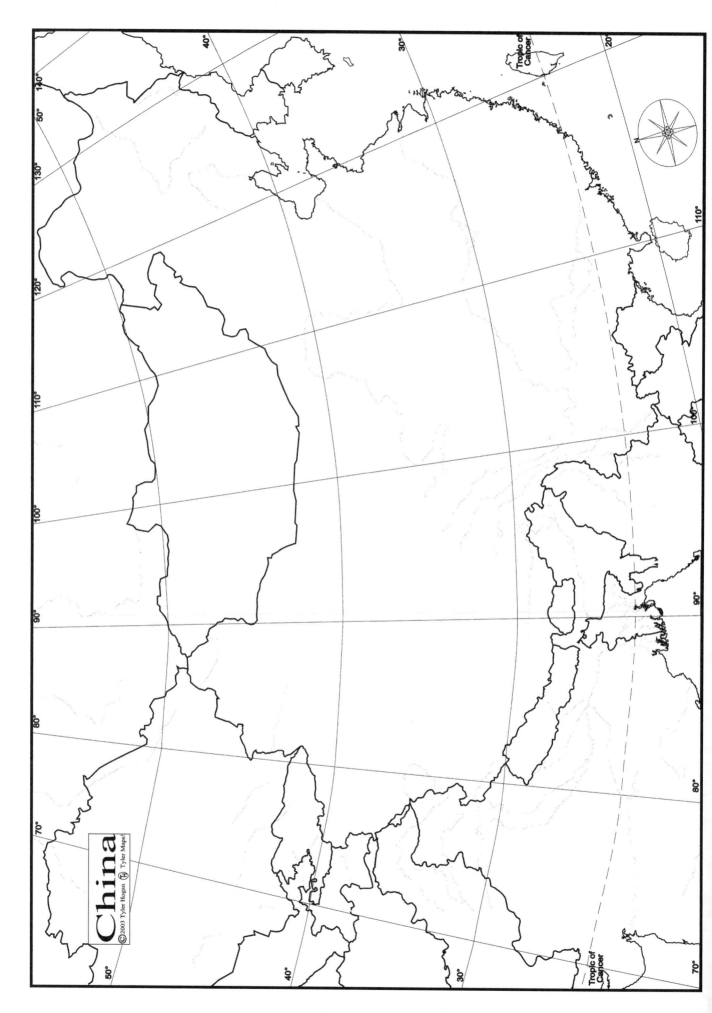

China

©2003 Tyler Hogan Ⓗ Tyler Maps

Tropic of Cancer

Tropic of Cancer

Tropic of Capricer

72

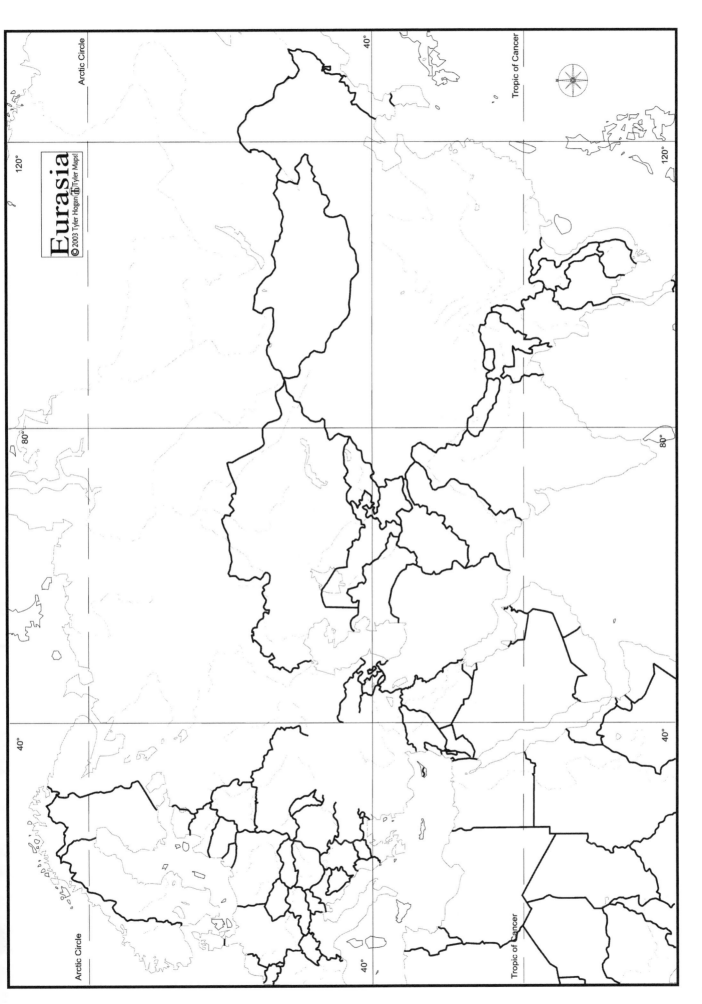

Eurasia

© 2003 Tyler Hogan (Tyler Maps)

Arctic Circle

120°

80°

40°

Tropic of Cancer

Arctic Circle

Tropic of Cancer

40°

80°

120°

40°

40°

GLOSSARY

Abacus   A hand-operated calculating machine in which numbers are represented by beads strung on wires or rods set in a rectangular frame. The Chinese most commonly use a *suan pan*, meaning "reckoning board."

Acupuncture   A form of traditional Chinese medicine in which needles are inserted at certain points or nerve centers along the body to relieve pain or cure certain diseases.

Alloy   A mixture of metals. Bronze is an example of an alloy; it is a mixture of copper and tin.

Antiseptics   Substances or processes that slow down or prevent the growth of germs.

Armillary sphere   An instrument that measures the positions of stars, like a protractor for the sky or a set of star rulers.

Bactrian camels   Camels that have two humps instead of one (as the dromedary has), making them more comfortable for riding. They survive the cold winter temperatures in the deserts of central Asia by growing extra-thick coats of fur in the fall.

Batten sails   Sails for Chinese junks that are made from bamboo mats stretched between poles so they can be lifted one piece at a time; the tight stretching lets the sail catch more wind.

Buddhism   The teachings of Buddha in India. Emphasis is on denying worldly desires to become "enlightened" and reach a state of nirvana.

Chlorophyll   The green photosynthetic coloring matter of plants. (Photosynthesis is the process by which a plant uses light to synthesize energy from carbon dioxide and water.)

Communism   An economic system and humanistic form of government in which all means of production—including land, natural resources, even families—are used by the government supposedly for the "good" of all its members.

Confucianism   The teachings of Confucius, which were a collection of principles for good government and personal behavior. Confucius lived in the 500 B.C. era.

Conscription   Forced time of service in an army.

Cormorants   Large, dark water birds with webbed feet and hooked bills, sometimes used for fishing on rivers in China.

Democracy   A government by the people, following the rule of the majority.

Dynasty   A series or succession of rulers from the same line of descent or a powerful group (often a family) that maintains its position for a considerable amount of time.

Ethnic group   A body of people with characteristics such as race, religion, or language in common.

Feudal system   The land in a region is owned by one ruler, but he makes grants of land to nobles in return for their military service.

Gunpowder   A mixture of charcoal, sulfur, and saltpeter that explodes when heated.

Halberds   Ax-like weapons of bronze with long wooden handles.

Hemp   A tall, weed-like plant; sometimes grown for its fibers, which are used for making cloth and rope.

Huns   Marauding tribes of Turkic and Tataric origins. The Huns later split into two groups, one of which was the Mongols that invaded China.

Hydroelectric   Electricity produced by water being channeled through a wheel-and-axle turbine to extract energy.

Incognito   In disguise or not recognized.

Jade   A hard gemstone that occurs in soft greens, grays, and browns. It has a smooth, satin-like finish when polished and was valued more than gold or silver in ancient China.

Junks   Ships from China with quilted or batten sails.

Kowtow The traditional Chinese way of showing great respect to a superior by kneeling before him and touching one's forehead to the ground.

Lodestone A rock that contains iron ore and attracts other metal objects.

Manchurians An ethnic group that lived in northeast China, but who were not Chinese. Manchus (or Manchurians) arrived as a barbarian tribe that broke through the Great Wall in 1644, and like the Mongols some 600 years before them, the Manchus set up their own dynasty.

Mandarin Mandarin actually comes from a Portuguese word used to denote any member of the imperial Chinese government. There were nine grades of rank in this civil service group which came into strength during the Tang dynasty.

Monsoon The periodic wind system that causes wet and dry weather in India and southern Asia. It comes from the Arabic word *mawsim*, which means "season."

Moxa (also known as **Moxibustion)** Treating patients for illnesses or pains by stimulating specific sites along the body with heat instead of needles (as in acupuncture).

Nirvana In Buddhism, an ideal condition of rest, harmony, stability or joy.

Opium A drug that finds its source in the opium poppy and that can change the brain of the opiate user so he does not feel pain because it blocks pain messages from reaching the brain. It can also change the brain so the user gets a feeling of pleasure, making him feel peaceful and sleepy.

Paddies Water-immersed fields used for growing rice.

Pagodas Far Eastern towers, often used as libraries or places of worship, and usually having roofs that curve upward at the division of each story.

Peking man An alleged fossil of a 690,000-year-old (or 7-million-year-old, depending on the source) man that was found near Beijing, China.

Pictograms A stylized picture or character used to represent things or concepts. The characters represent entire words, not merely sounds. *Picto* comes from the Latin word *pictura*, meaning "painting." *Gram* comes from the Greek word *gramma*, meaning "letter" or "something written down."

Porcelain Fine pottery, actually a cross between glass and pottery.

Republic A country with an elected government rather than one ruled by a monarch or king/queen.

Rickshaw (or *jinriksha* in its full name) is a small, two-wheeled carriage drawn usually by one person.

Sampans Boats in China with huts onboard.

Sedan chair is an enclosed chair carried on poles by two or four men.

Seismograph A machine developed in A.D. 130 that could detect an earthquake and indicate its direction from China's capital at that time, Loyang.

Silk road The overland trade route from Rome, Italy, to China. It consisted of some 2,500 miles of road for trading goods between East and West.

Steppes Vast, level, treeless tracts of arid land in southeastern Europe and Asia.

Surname The name family members have in common.

Tangram A Chinese game in which various pictures are made from a square divided into seven pieces.

Taoism The religion based on Lao Tzu's philosophy. It encourages harmony with nature, living and working together peacefully, and meditation.

Vaccination The introduction of a small amount of a virus so that the body will develop an immunity to that virus.

Xanadu Kublai Khan's summer palace in northern China, on the border of Mongolia.

Yin and yang Two alleged forces in nature that the Chinese believe need to be kept in balance. They are symbolized by a circle of interlocking black and white halves. *Yin* is the dark, feminine, and weaker force. *Yang* is the lighter, male, and stronger force.

Yurt A circular, domed portable tent used by the nomadic Mongols.

BIBLIOGRAPHY

Aliki. *Mummies Made in Egypt*. Mexico: Harper Collins Publishers, 1979. Describes the techniques and reasons for use of mummification in ancient Egypt. Use it for comparison with the burial process of Shang kings during the same timeframe. ISBN 0064460118.

Allison, Amy. *Life in Ancient China*. San Diego, CA: Lucent Books, 2001. Primarily focusing on life in China during the Han dynasty, this book presents cultural and historical information through text and periodic black and white illustrations or photos. Allison reveals what homes were like in ancient China, how classes were ranked, what goods were traded, and other interesting daily life details. The occasional highlight boxes with research on etiquette, kites, morality, bachelor life, and so forth are equally intriguing. Excellent resource for answering student questions. (For ages 10+ because of the amount of text, unless used for short passages or specific information.) Dewey # J 931.04 AL438L. ISBN 1560066946.

Ames, Lee J. *Draw 50 Boats, Ships, Trucks and Trains*. Garden City, NY: Doubleday, 1976. Step-by-step illustrations help budding artists draw a variety of forms of transportation. The Chinese-junk artwork is particularly appropriate for the China unit. Dewey # J 743 Ame. ISBN 0385089031.

Anthony, Susan. *FACTS Plus: An Almanac of Essential Information*. Anchorage, AK: Instructional Resources Company, 1992. Dewey # 031.02 Ant. ISBN 187947803X.

Armentrout, David, and Armentrout, Patricia. *Treasures from Ancient China*. Vero Beach, FL: Rourke Book Company, 2001. Very short chapters on different dynasties and unique elements of Chinese history, usually accompanied by full-page color photos. Pronunciation aids throughout *and* at the back of the book, but the book is not overly informative. (For ages 5–10.) Dewey # J 931 Arm. ISBN 1559162880.

Arquilevich, Gabriel. *Fairview's Guide to Composition and Essay Writing*. Oak View, CA: Fairview Publishing, 1998. This resource comes from the viewpoint that essay writing and composition are *creative* acts; they are not meant to be dry, stereotypical, molded, five-paragraph-only, introduction and "in conclusion" bookended writings. Mr. Arquilevich exhorts students (ideally in grades 9–12) to keep a reading journal of a variety of authors and essay styles, which will enhance their own creative efforts in their essays. He discusses tone, audience, paragraphing, introductions and conclusions, brainstorming, drafting, sentence fluidity (word choice, transitions, quote incorporation), sentence combining, and four types of essays (taking a stand, compare and contrast, personal, and mock/imitative)—offering different activities and assignments for applying the information presented to the reader. Answers to some of the exercises are provided, but because many of the assignments are based on personal topic choices, answers will vary. The guide encourages using peer editing in small-group situations, making it a good co-op resource for high school writers; however, Mr. Arquilevich addresses how the guide can be used in a self-directed, homeschooling situation, as well. ISBN 0964904217.

Beshore, George. *Science in Ancient China*. New York: Franklin Watts (Grolier Publishing), 1998. Chapters cover ancient Chinese science, alchemy, medicine, astronomy, and mathematics. Explanations are not exceptionally detailed, but they do provide good introductions to the numerous science-related discoveries for which we have the Chinese to thank. (Ages 6–14.) Dewey # J 951.01 Bes. ISBN 0531159140.

Buck, Pearl. *The Man Who Changed China*. New York: Random House, 1953. In 1911, Sun Yat-sen, leader of the Kuomintang (National People's Party), led the Chinese to overthrow the weakened Manchu rulers and to establish a republic. Pearl Buck wrote a book entitled *The Man Who Changed China* for the Landmark series. While it is well written stylistically, its content sometimes aggrandizes Sun Yat-sen. His own family life testifies that he was not the saint that Buck tends to emphasize. Nevertheless, Sun Yat-sen's charisma and the dynamics of the revolution that he encouraged in China are clearly presented in this book. LCCN 53-6263.

Burnie, David. *The Kingfisher Illustrated Animal Encyclopedia*. New York: Kingfisher, 2000. Provides exceptional color photographs plus short paragraph explanations of hundreds of animals from around the world. ISBN 0753452839.

Clarke, Donald. *The Encyclopedia of How It Works from Abacus to Zoom Lens*. New York: A & W Publishers, Inc., 1977. Provides an excellent explanation of how an abacus is used for calculations. Dewey # Q 620 C551E. ISBN 0894790021.

Cotterell, Arthur. *Ancient China* (Eyewitness Books Series). New York: Dorling Kindersley (Alfred Knopf), 1994. Phenomenal photos of items, models, paintings, and so forth, all related to the culture and history of ancient China. Captions are a wealth of information. Surprisingly, not evolutionary, but also nonjudgmental on religions and mysticism of the realm. Very interesting and useful, answering many of those student-generated statements that start with "I wonder why . . ." (For all ages.) Dewey # J 931 Cot. ISBN 067986167X.

DeJong, Meindert. *The House of Sixty Fathers*. New York: HarperCollins Publications Inc., 1956. A moving story of Tien Pao's escape from the Japanese army's invasion into China. His courage and persistence impress the 60 American airmen who "adopt" him until he can find his family. A good read-aloud book, but tenderhearted youngsters may be disturbed by the tragedies and difficulties the young hero endures. (Tien Pao also prays to the river god, so some discussion on the True God versus idols will be necessary.) Set in the year 1931, this is a Newbery Honor winner for readers ages 9–14. ISBN 0064402002.

Demi. *Happy New Year! Kung-Hsi Fa-Ts'ai!* New York: Crown Publishers, Inc., 1997. ISBN 0517885921.
Demi. *Kites*. New York: Crown Publishers, Inc., 1999. ISBN 0375810080.
These books reveal the symbolism or association made with various plants and animals praised by the Chinese and provide history on the use of kites, information on the Chinese zodiac, and cultural traditions from China. Be aware, however, that these books do not judge Chinese mysticism in any manner. (For ages 5–9.)

DeStafano, Susan. *Focus on Opiates*. Frederick, MD: Twenty-First Century Books, 1991. This book for fifth and sixth graders explains how opiates can be used for healing or for harm. Portions of Chapters 3 and 4 (up to page 40) are really the only sections I would recommend because they focus on the scientific and biological effects that opiates have on the brain. The rest of the book sometimes seems to make excuses for an addict's sin. Dewey # J362.29. ISBN 0941477916.

Dramer, Kim. *Games People Play: China*. New York: Children's Press (Grolier Publishing), 1997. Discusses the entertainment options of Chinese children from ancient to modern times. History of and rules for the various games, toys, and sports are explained. (Ages 7–11.) Dewey # J 790.09 Dra. ISBN 0516203088.

Ferroa, Peggy. *Cultures of the World: China*. New York: Marshall Cavendish, 1991. Mostly focusing on modern culture in China, but the cultural and societal influences from dynastic eras are well explained. Interesting information on language, the arts, foods, and holidays. Colorful photos help convey life in current China and how an average Chinese family enjoys life in Eastern Asia. (Lots of text, so best for gathering resource information or for ages 11+.) Dewey # YP 951 Fer. ISBN 1854353993.

Fisher, Leonard Everett. *The Great Wall of China*. New York: Simon & Schuster, 1986. A young-reader book chronicling Qin emperor Shih Huang-Ti's intent to build a wall to stop Mongolian invasions. The magnitude of this feat, the construction process, later improvements made in the Ming dynasty, and Chinese characters and "chops" on every other page add to the cultural feel and details of this 30-page study. (Ages 5–10.) ISBN 068901785.

Flack, Marjorie and Wiese, Kurt. *The Story About Ping*. New York: Viking Press, 1933. Follow Ping's adventures on the Yangtze River one day when he is separated from his family. (The adventures are doubly unique because Ping is a duck.) Dewey # JE-Fla. ISBN 0670672238.

Gelman, Rita Golden. *Rice Is Life*. New York: Henry Holt & Company, 2000. An interesting book about the *process* of growing and harvesting rice, but it is set on the island of Bali, below China. That geographical distinction and the difference between a paddy and a *sawah* may confuse some children; still, the discussion on the eels, dragonflies, bats, mice, and other critters that are "involved" in rice production is fascinating. *Rice Is Life* also presents another opportunity for thanking our God that He is the one True God to Whom we should express our gratitude for His provision in our lives! Dewey # J 633.18 GeL. ISBN 0805057196.

Goldstein, Peggy. *Long is a Dragon*. San Francisco, CA: China Books & Periodicals, Inc., 1991. It is subtitled "Chinese Writing for Children" and encourages them to practice writing sample characters provided in the book. It also explains pronunciation of Chinese words. A simple illustration of an idea or a word transitions into the corresponding Chinese pictogram, which helps the ideograph "make sense" visually. (For ages 5-12, but it offers good information for older students as well.) Dewey #495.1 GoL. ISBN 0835123758.

Hansen, Henny H. *Mongol Costumes*. Farnborough Hampshire, England: Thames & Hudson, 1994. Provides colorful illustrations of Mongolian fashions from various eras. Use this resource for tracing costumes or drawing clothing from Genghis Khan's time. ISBN 0500015856.

Haskins, Jim. *Count Your Way Through China*. Minneapolis: Carolrhoda Books, Inc., 1987. Learn to count from 1 to 10 in Mandarin, as well as how to write these numbers in pictogram form and how to pronounce them. Brief cultural or historical information is also supplied with each number. The number 2, for instance, is represented by two giant pandas—Ling-Ling and Hsing-Hsing—which the People's Republic of China gave the United States in 1972. (For ages 5–10.) Dewey # J 951 Has. ISBN 0876144865.

Herbert, Janis. *Marco Polo for Kids*. Chicago: Chicago Review Press, 2001. If you want a ton of activity ideas for the Yuan dynasty, Ms. Herbert has developed 21 of them for you, in addition to biographical and historical material. The recipe for making terra-cotta clay (p. 35) is very useful for the Qin unit, as well. Our disclaimer for this book is that some of the suggested activities make no judgment on the beliefs and religious views of most Chinese, and some ideas on evolution are proposed as fact. Some exercises include the mysticism of feng shui, yoga, and qigong, for example. We'd recommend that you read aloud (and discuss) the portions of text you wish to use so that your children are not innocently confused by the material on the Dali Lama, Java Man, and so forth. (For ages 5–14.) ISBN 1556523777.

Hippocrene Children's Illustrated Chinese (Mandarin) Dictionary. New York: Hippocrene Books, Inc., 2001. The dictionary provides colorful illustrations (from airplane to zebra), pictographs, and pronunciations for a variety of words. English to Chinese and Chinese to English listings are both given. Dewey #J 495.1 Hip. ISBN 0781808340 or 0781808480.

Hong, Lily Toy. *The Empress and the Silkworm*. Morton Grove, IL: Albert Whitman & Company, 1995. Fictionalized rendition of Empress Si Ling-Chi's discovery of using silkworm cocoons for making shiny cloth. This allegedly occurred around 2700 B.C., and this simple young reader gives a good introduction to life under the Emperor Huang-Ti. (For ages 5–9.) Dewey # J 677.39 Hon. ISBN 0807520098.

Hughes-Stanton, Penelope. *See Inside an Ancient Chinese Town*. Danbury, CT: Franklin Watts, 1986. Through text and colorful illustrations, readers are shown inside the protective walls of the capital city of Loyang from the Han empire in A.D. 25. From the nobleman's house to the marketplace, and even to burial customs and religious thought, *See Inside* proffers good introductory material for younger students. Unique timeline in back traces events in China, Asia, Europe, and the Near East from 3500 B.C. to A.D. 907. (Ages 5–11.) Dewey # J 931 Hug. ISBN 0521190099.

Hull, Edward. *The Wall Chart of World History*. New York: Barnes & Noble Bookstores, 1989. An oversized, fold-out timeline of world history, from a refreshingly biblical and creationist viewpoint. It seems convoluted and confusing, initially, but it really helps you track who lived when. It also indicates major events and government changes in the different cultures of the world. You'll be impressed by how minuscule America's history is in comparison to the overall history of the world. An excellent reference resource for "jumping-off" points in a unit study. (For reference.) ISBN 0880292393.

Jensen, Frode. *Jensen's Format Writing*. Grants Pass, OR: Wordsmiths, 2002. Jensen's work is designed to teach expository writing to high schoolers. Its primary purpose is to teach writers how to organize sentences into paragraphs, paragraphs into essays, and how to gather information and document it. Includes lots of helpful tips for teachers/parents about how to assist and evaluate their students' writing; additionally, it has check sheets for grading assignments and tests, answer keys, and sample schedules to consider when giving writing assignments. Essay types covered include example, classification, definition, process, analogy, cause/effect, and comparison. ISBN 1886061297.

Jiang, Ji-li. *Red Scarf Girl*. New York: HarperCollins, 1997. An autobiographical account of Ji-li Jiang's life in the early years of the Cultural Revolution. The confusion created by Mao Zedong's oppression and brainwashing is haunting. It's not a difficult read in terms of the concepts it presents; in fact, it presents elements of Communism and modern Chinese culture in a manner that makes them more comprehensible and memorable than any other resource I've encountered. However, because of some expletives (used in dialogue between the Red Guards and "black" Chinese, who were opponents of Communism), descriptions of violent actions taken against the blacks, and vague religious views that need discussion, I would say *Red Scarf Girl* is for upper elementary students. (For ages 11+.) Dewey # J 951.05 Jia. ISBN 0060275855.

Kapit, Wynn. *The Geography Coloring Book*. New York: Addison-Wesley Educational Publishers Inc., 1999. The color-coded method covered in this geography study tool makes it an excellent reference resource for older students. Detailed maps require fine motor-skill control for coloring precisely. Area, population, the capital, government system, language, religion, exports and climate, and unique historical notes for each country are included. This supplemental information makes the book an excellent reference resource for all students and teachers. ISBN 0321032810.

Kingfisher History Encyclopedia, The. New York: Larousse Kingfisher Chambers, 1999. Dewey 909. ISBN 0753451948.
Kingfisher Illustrated History of the World, The. New York: Larousse Kingfisher Chambers, 1993. Dewey 909. ISBN 1856978621.
Both books provide great background information and interesting tidbits of cultural and historical data. Evolutionary worldview initially, but on track after 4000 B.C. In *Illustrated History of the World,* some two-page spreads on the different dynasties are very interesting and helpful for quick springboard ideas. A running timeline helps you trace what else was happening in the world at the same time as the dynasties. While the continuous annotated timeline is missing in *History Encyclopedia*, the rest of the content is essentially the same as the 1993 edition of the book. Excellent indexes! (Reference resource of for ages 10+.)

Koenig, Marion. *The Travels of Marco Polo* (Adventures from History). New York: Golden Press, Inc., 1964. An exceptional introductory book on life in China during Kublai Khan's reign and a chronological explanation of Polo's travels in the mid-13th century. Well told, including memorable fables, tales, and cultural notes from countries other than Cathay. The front interior map chronicling Polo's journeys is unmatched in any other resource I've seen. (For ages 5–14 reading aloud or for ages 10–14 reading alone.)

Komroff, Manuel. *Marco Polo*. Englewood Cliffs, NJ: Julian Messner, 1952, or New York: Simon & Schuster, 1967. Reads more like historical fiction than "history." (It is reminiscent of Landmark titles in that regard.) Chapters are usually only 5 to 10 pages in length and follow a chronological format. Excellent discussion of the Kublai Khan's summer residence, Xanadu; the political intrigue in his own court; and the events leading to the Polos' return to Italy. (For ages 5–14 reading aloud or for ages 9+ reading alone.) Dewey # YPB POLO.

Lamb, Harold. *Genghis Khan and the Mongol Horde*. New York: Random House, 1954. Yes, it's a Landmark title written by the author of *Tales from Shakespeare*. Genghis Khan and his ferocious tribe of Mongols conquered China, Iran, Russia, and Mongolia. His conquests overthrew the barriers of the Dark Ages and established contact between Asia and Europe. Excellent read-aloud chapter book or for upper elementary readers. One note: "Christian" is used rather vaguely for nearly any European religion. Holds the interest of good readers while hooking reluctant ones! (Ages 5–14.) Dewey # JB Genghis Khan. LCCN 54-5164. ISBN 0208022872.

Lamb, Harold. *Genghis Khan: The Emperor of All Men*. Garden City, NY: Garden City Publishing Co., Inc., 1927. A very readable but detailed study of Genghis Khan's life and accomplishments. Wonderfully researched, but it reads like historical fiction rather than dry history. Index could allow for related excerpts to be read to younger students at appropriate times. (Ages 15+.)

Lazo, Caroline. *The Terra Cotta Army of Emperor Qin*. New York: New Discovery Books, 1993. The title explains exactly what the book is about: the 7,500 life-size clay figures buried near Xian, China, at the First Emperor's tomb. Great insight into life in the Qin dynasty and the archaeological treasures uncovered in 1974. A bit dry in places (not just because of the terra-cotta, either) but memorable because this was such an amazing archaeological discovery. (Ages 5–14.) Dewey # J 931.04 Laz. ISBN 0027546314.

Macaulay, David. *The New Way Things Work*. Boston: Houghton Mifflin, 1998. David Macaulay (of *Castle, Pyramid, City*, etc., fame) has simply and clearly explained the scientific principles and workings of hundreds of machines through his delightful illustrations and comprehensible text. Nearly 400 pages of text and illustrations cover everything from the inclined plane to the Internet. The book is arranged in five sections of study: the mechanics of movement, harnessing the elements, working with waves, electricity and automation, and the digital domain. Moreover, it includes a chapter on when certain machines were invented, a division on technical terms, and an extensive index. Any age of learner will enjoy this book—whether it's used for research or for entertainment! Dewey # J 600 Mac. ISBN 0395938473.

Macdonald, Fiona. *Marco Polo: A Journey Through China*. New York: Grolier (Franklin Watts), 1997. A highly illustrated, simple introduction to the expeditions and discoveries of Italy's Marco Polo. The colorful illustrations, historical and geographical sidebars, and interesting cultural notes make this a good introductory book for deeper studies into Marco Polo's impact on world travel. (For ages 5–10.) ISBN 0531153401.

MacLenighan, Valjean. *Enchantment of the World: China*. Chicago, IL: Children's Press, 1983. Basically a geographical and historical study of the country of China for older elementary and junior high students. It is somewhat dry in its text, but it provides excellent chronological information, and it has interesting captions under its illustrations and photos. Dewey #J 951 Mac. ISBN 0516027549.

Mah, Adeline Yen. *Chinese Cinderella: The True Story of an Unwanted Daughter*. New York: Delacorte Press, 1999. The autobiography of a 20th century Chinese daughter who is obviously unwanted by her father and new stepmother. Some of the conflict, treatment, and strained family relationships are influenced by Communist brainwashing, so this is an intriguing (though haunting) study of life in a Chinese family during the Communist regime. Dewey # YP B Mah. ISBN 0385327072.

Marden, Patricia, and Barchers, Suzanne. *Cooking Up World History*. Westport, CT: Libraries Unlimited, 1994. More than 20 countries and regions are introduced through the recipes, research, readings, and related media recommendations offered in this tasty resource. Each chapter contains a brief introduction describing the cookery of a culture, five or six recipes that provide a complete meal, research questions that connect the culture and food to history, and annotated bibliographies of additional reading resources and media supplements. ISBN 1563081164.

Martell, Hazel. *Imperial China*. Austin, TX: Raintree Steck-Vaughn Publishers, 1999. Covering the period from 221 B.C. to A.D. 1294, easily understood text and full-color pictures explain key characters, events, ideas, inventions, beliefs, and dynastic changes of the period from the first emperor to Kublai Khan's death. Sometimes the material almost triggers more questions than it answers, but the pronunciation key at the end is very helpful. (For ages 10–12 or for brief explanations for younger children.) Dewey # J 951.01 Mar. ISBN 0817254250.

McKinney, Kevin. *Everyday Geography*. Chicago: Contemporary Books, 1994. Over 80 maps and illustrations added to very readable, interesting text give you a wonderful geography resource. Maps are simple but clear, and could be colored if desired. Fun "geofacts" are scattered throughout and periodic quizzes help readers review facts they've learned. The book covers the seven continents by countries and islands. ISBN 0809235501.

Mosel, Arlene. *Tikki Tikki Tembo*. New York: Henry Holt, 1968. A light-hearted look at how Chinese children have come to have short names, which also provides a fun peek into Chinese culture. For younger children (ages 3–10). Dewey # J 398 Mos. ISBN 0805006621.

National Geographic Society. *Journey Into China*. Washington, DC: National Geographic Society, 1982. The amazing photographs you would expect from a National Geographic title; unfortunately, the evolutionary stance you'd expect from the NGS, as well. Chapters are divided by China's geographical regions, so the photos are ideal for the geography unit of this study—even though most are of modern life within the context of China's history and culture. (For all ages.) Dewey # 915.10457. ISBN 0870444379.

O'Connor, Jane. *The Emperor's Silent Army.* New York: Penguin Putnam, 2002. A simple but fascinating book about the terra-cotta warriors of the first emperor of China, Qin Shih Huang-Ti. Until 1974, modern man didn't know that these 7,500 terra-cotta replicas of the Qin's army existed. A major, ongoing archaeological dig outside Xian—chronicled here in large, color photos and text—is revealing more about life in China more than 2,200 years ago. It is considered as significant a find as those in the great pyramids of Egypt. (For ages 6–12, especially.) ISBN 0670035122.

Pak, Amy. *History Through the Ages Historical Timeline Figures.* Holley, NY: Home School in the Woods, 2002 and 2003. These timeline figures provide gorgeous detailed illustrations with a short mini-paragraph of text that supply the date and a brief description of the person or event being depicted. Mrs. Pak is a professional illustrator, so the pictures are lovely. Even when these figures are reduced to 65% of their original size the text can be read clearly. Students can color the figures and attach them in the appropriate place on the timelines provided with each packet of figures, or create their own timeline notebooks. Three sets of timeline figures are available: "Creation to Christ" (250 images); "Resurrection to the Revolution" (250 images) covering the period from 0 to 1799 A.D. (including the fall of Rome, the Middle Ages, Renaissance and Reformation, and the Age of Enlightenment); and the "American History" packet (420 images) covering a period from the Explorers to the 21st century.

Perry, Ellen, and Topping, Audrey. *Great Wall Across the Yangtze.* PBS Home Videos, 2000. A 60-minute video that investigates the changes the Three Gorges Dam project will bring to China's environment, history, and people. The video was made without Chinese government authorization and thoroughly examines this 15-year project for creating the world's largest dam and hydroelectric power plant. Dewey # VHS 951 Chi.

Polo, Marco. (Marsden, William, translator.) *The Travels of Marco Polo, the Venetian.* Any edition. Why not have your older students (ages 14+) help out with your research of Polo's travels by reading his dictated autobiography? Not an easy read, but fascinating and a great study in Chinese history, culture, and geography.

Powell, Jillian. *Everyone Eats Rice.* Austin, TX: Raintree Steck-Vaughn, 1997. A simple book that explains the parts of a rice plant; the known history of rice; how it is grown, harvested, and prepared; and the significance of rice in different cultures. Dewey # J 641.33 Pow. ISBN 0817247580.

Reader's Digest Video and Television. *Imperial Splendors.* Pleasantville, NY: Reader's Digest Video, 1996. Approximately a 60-minute video that provides almost ten minutes each of film footage of both Xanadu (Kublai Khan's summer palace) and the Forbidden City. Dewey # VHS 912 Gre.

Richardson, Adele. *Silk.* Mankato, MN: Creative Education, 2000. This colorful photojournalistic-style young reader is a clear presentation of silk production and use. Very elementary, but unusual, facts included in the text are interesting. (Ages 5–10.) Dewey # J 6777.39 Ric. ISBN 0886829631.

Saddington, Marianne. *Making Your Own Paper.* Pownal, VT: Storey Communications, 1992. More extravagant and creative forms of papermaking are presented in this craft book. ISBN 0882667858.

Sebranek, Patrick, Kemper, Dave, and Meyer, Verne. *Writer's Inc.* Wilmington, MA: Houghton Mifflin, 2001. This book goes far beyond "merely" educating us on aspects of the writing process. It is intended for high school students through adults, and it includes sections on speaking, root words, grammar, geography, measurement, almanac information, and much more. "Reference manual" best describes this book. ISBN 0669471860.

Shifeng, Zheng, et al. *China.* New York: McGraw-Hill Book Company, 1980. Fantastic photographs of all the provinces and peoples in China. Informative captions and pages of text between mounds of photos provide more detailed material about the history, geography, and culture of China. Striking pictures (in a saddening way) of Buddhist idols and temples, which are especially appropriate for study of the Han and Sui dynasties. (For all ages.) Dewey # 915.1 Chi. ISBN 00705608308.

Shuter, Jane. *The Ancient Chinese* (History Opens Windows Series). Des Plaines, IL: Heinemann Interactive Library, 1998. A very simple introduction to China—from life along the Yellow River to the Mongolian invasion under Genghis Khan. There *is* a belief in evolution promoted at the beginning of the book. Colorful photos and illustrations grace each page, but the text is elementary and general. (Ages 5–7.) Dewey # J DS 721.S488. ISBN 1575725940.

Steele, Philip. *Step Into the Chinese Empire.* New York: Lorenz Books (Anness Publishing Limited), 1998. A cross between an Eyewitness book (with lots of photos/illustrations, plus informative captions) and a craft book on ancient China. Homes, occupations, foods, inventions, clothing, and more are briefly explained with text and illustrations, and related crafts are periodically presented. Some of these crafts include models of sampans and pagodas, Tang armor, kite making, printing blocks, etc. (Style and text suitable for ages 7–12, but crafts mostly for ages 10+, if attempted alone.) Dewey # J 951 Ste. ISBN 1859677622.

Stenuf, T.J. *Pulp and Paper.* North Brunswick, NJ: The Scouts, 1980. Explains the process of making paper fairly simply. Dewey # J 369.43 Boy.

Stone, Lynn. *The Provinces and Cities of China.* Vero Beach, FL: Rourke Book Company, Inc., 2001. Simple text and full-page photographs reveal the independent regions and major cities of modern China. Not exceptionally fascinating but "to the point." (Ages 5–9.) Dewey # J 951 Sto. ISBN 1559163208.

Sun, Ming-Ju. *Chinese Fashions Coloring Book.* Mineola, NY: Dover Publications, Inc., 2002. Supplies images of over 1000 years of fashion, from the Tang dynasty (618-907) to the Republic period (1911-1949). Men's and women's fashions, as well as hairstyles, are presented. Some explanation is also provided on the common symbols, fabric choices, and key fashion influences in the different dynasties. ISBN 0486420531.

Tao, Wang. *Exploration Into China.* Parsippany, NJ: New Discovery Books, 1995. Very much an evolutionary introduction in the book, and sometimes the layout seems choppy in presentation. But interesting tidbits of information, some of which are not presented in other works on ancient China. (The material on Chinese historical figures, in particular, is verifiable, and interesting.) More of a reference resource than a smooth read. (Ages 7–12.) Dewey # J 951 Wan. ISBN 00271880875.

Vine, W.E. *Vine's Complete Expository Dictionary of Old and New Testament Words*. Nashville, TN: Thomas Nelson Publishers, 1996. ISBN 0899576699.

Walsh, Richard. *Adventures and Discoveries of Marco Polo* (Landmark Series). New York: Random House, 1953. Walsh does a wonderful job of presenting Polo's adventures and experiences with the Kublai Khan in an exciting but readable style. Quoted matter is from Marsden's translation of Polo's own book. Index in the back is helpful, and the book just makes a great chapter read-aloud choice for the Yuan dynasty. (For ages 5–14 reading aloud or for ages 10–14 reading alone.) LCCN 53-6270.

Williams, Brian. *See Through History: Ancient China.* New York: Viking Publishers, 1996. Two-page layouts of pictures, photos, captions, and text provide material from ancient civilization to present day. Some evolutionary content at the beginning. Several illustrations have transparent overlays that allow readers to "see through" the interior of a Shang tomb or a Han nobleman's house, for instance. (For ages 5–12.) Dewey # J 951 WiL. ISBN 0670871575.

Williams, Suzanne. *Made in China*. Berkeley, CA: Pacific View Press, 1996. Clear layout with interesting text and colorful illustrations provides decent introduction to ideas and inventions from ancient China. Using a chronological approach, advancements and changes in each era are explained succinctly but memorably. Not cluttered; has genuinely interesting side notes that youngsters will enjoy. (Ages 6–12.) Dewey # J 951 WiL. ISBN 18881896145.

Wolff, Diane. *Chinese Writing*. New York: Holt, Rinehart & Winston, 1975. Offers a fairly simple introduction to the characteristics of written and spoken Chinese, as well as a discussion of Chinese calligraphy and instructions for writing characters. A bit dry, but clear and informative for ages 11 and up. Dewey #J 495.1 Wol. ISBN 0030130069.

Young, Ed. *Monkey King*. New York: HarperCollins Publishers, 2001. Sun Wukong (the Monkey King), who was a "heavenly being," accompanied his master to India searching for the Buddhist religious scriptures, the Tripitaka. His clever, cunning, acrobatic, sometimes mischievous character had a good heart, and he was always devoted to the traveling monk. Ed Young's young reader (doubly so, considering the author's last name) is a simplified retelling of the original epic, but it makes no judgment on Buddhist beliefs or gods, so discussion on what is *truth* will definitely need to be included. Dewey # JP-You. ISBN 0060279192.

Yu, Ling. *Cooking the Chinese Way*. Minneapolis, MN: Lerner Publications Company, 1982. Chinese cooking fundamentals—techniques, utensils, special ingredients, and chopstick instructions—all precede recipes of classic Chinese fare. Recipe names in Chinese are also provided, allowing for your own Chinese restaurant with "real menus." (Ages 5+.) Dewey # J 641.5 Yu. ISBN 0822509024.

Zacharias, Ravi. *The Lotus and the Cross: Jesus Talks with Buddha*. Sisters, OR: Multnomah Publishers, 2001. Mr. Zacharias offers an unusual approach to comparing the truth of the gospel with the religious views of Buddha by writing an imagined conversation between Jesus and Buddha. Best for high schoolers and adults. ISBN 157673854X.

Zhang, Song Nan. *A Little Tiger in the Chinese Night*. Plattsburgh, NY: Tundra Books, 1993. This is another one of those hauntingly engrossing autobiographies. Written by an artist who survived Mao Tse-tung's horrific Cultural Revolution in China, the author/illustrator relates his experiences from 1945 up through one-and-a-half years after the Tiananmen Square uprising. Full-page, full-color illustrations accompany the thrilling, joyous, heartbreaking, terrifying, and ultimately victorious account when he and his family reunite in Montreal, Canada. His love for his country and his people, in spite of the pain he endured under Chairman Mao's regime, is touching and unwavering. The historical timeline in the back of the book provides a great history lesson on *why* China was so susceptible to Tse-tung's brainwashing in the 20th century. (For upper elementary and junior high students, although this title could be used as a read-aloud with younger children. Please use discretion, ignoring or editing pages that may be too poignant for your tenderhearted children.) ISBN 0887763561.

Additional Resources
Books

Ganeri, Anita. *What Would You Ask Marco Polo?* London: Thameside Press, 1999. Question and answer interview format sets up short summaries of historical details about Polo's travels. Very simple but good historical timeline, glossary, and index. (Ages 5–9.) Dewy # J 915.042092. ISBN 1929298005.

Grun, Bernard. *The Timetables of History*. New York: Simon & Schuster, 1991. An easy-to-use reference tool—from its detailed index, to its yearly charts—and it begins from a believable time frame (5000–4001 B.C.). It helps readers comprehend what was occurring at given points in history by reading brief summaries of events in each of the following categories: History/Politics, Literature and Theater, Religion/Philosophy and Learning, Visual Arts, Music, Science/Technology and Growth, and Daily Life. *The Timetables of History* makes it a cinch to create timelines of interest and relevance to what you're studying. It's a good "jumping-off-point" resource for any history unit study. ISBN 067174271X.

Hatcher, Carolyn. *Let the Authors Speak*. Joelton, TN: Old Pinnacle Publishing, 1992. A reference book for guiding you to "worthy books" based on historical setting. By "historical setting" we mean the century or location of the story in any of the nearly 1,300 books Hatcher lists. Reading levels and interest levels are provided for most titles. Brief comments as to the content, availability, style, and so forth of each book are also given. Listings begin with Greek, Roman, and Middle Eastern times, and continue to the present. Excellent reference resource for any homeschool family but particularly for those using the unit study approach. ISBN 0964068117.

Lima, Carolyn, and Lima, John. *A to Zoo: Subject Access to Children's Picture Books*. Westport, CT: Bowker-Greenwood, 2001. A good resource for finding picture books and simple young-reader books on a multitude of different subjects. It does not come from a Christian perspective, so you will not always agree with every suggestion, but it simplifies the search process substantially. Dewey # J R 011.62 Lim. ISBN 0313320691.

Roth, Susan L.. *Marco Polo: His Notebook*. New York: Doubleday, 1990. Fictionalized diary entries, as though written by Marco Polo during his 20 years of travel in Cathay. Ideas are based on actual events from Polo's book, *The Travels of Marco Polo*, but very much using modern syntax and worldviews. Not "a winner," but a fast overview of Polo's remarkable travels if you're exceptionally limited on time. (Ages 5–9.) Dewey # J B Polo. ISBN 038526495X.

Smith, Bradley, and Weng, Wan-go. *China: A History in Art*. New York: Harper & Row, 1976. Rich, full-color photos of art from ancient China to the 20th century. Some evolutionary thought contained in text and captions, but the photos cannot be rivaled—except perhaps by a field trip to your nearest museum. (For all ages.) Dewey # 915.103 Sm52c. ISBN 0060139323.

Wilson, Elizabeth. *Books Children Love: A Guide to the Best Children's Literature*. Wheaton, IL: Crossway Books, 1987. This book is a treasure chest of "living books" information. The main purpose of this book is to recommend books in nearly 25 different subject areas. A short paragraph annotating the recommended titles, along with grade level listings and the publishers, is also included. It is written by a Christian author, so you can trust her choices and reasons more readily. ISBN 0891074414.

Websites

China Online
(From the "What You Need to Know About" site)
http://chineseculture.about.com/cs/aboutchina/
Provides basic information about China's geography, climate, provinces, population, ethnic groups, religions and more. It also has articles by topic about Chinese festivals, names, foods, games, traditions, legends, and so forth. Maps of China, Taiwan, and Hong Kong are available through this site.

China Page
http://www.chinapage.com/china.html
Over 40 topics related to China are listed at this site, covering everything from astronomy to water projects. Its focus is on classical Chinese art, painting, calligraphy, poetry, literature, history, and philosophy. Helpful subtopics for this unit study include the articles on the chronology of emperors, sayings of Confucius, the sound of the Chinese language, Chinese words, and Admiral Zheng He's naval expeditions.

Enchanted Learning
http://www.enchantedlearning.com/asia/china/
Ideal for children in the younger grades, it supplies simple material about China and its culture. It also has an outline map of China's major cities and landmarks, with a quiz corresponding to the map. (For grades K-3, especially.)

Index

Other Quality Books from Zeezok Publishing

The Shining Sword
When I'm a Daddy
When I'm a Mommy

From the Great Composers Series
by Opal Wheeler and Sybil Deucher

Sebastian Bach, The Boy from Thuringia
Ludwig Beethoven and the Chiming Tower Bells
Mozart, The Wonder Boy
Handel at the Court of Kings
Joseph Haydn, The Merry Little Peasant
Robert Schumann and Mascot Ziff
Franz Schubert and His Merry Friends
Frederic Chopin, Son of Poland, Early Years
Frederic Chopin, Son of Poland, Later Years
Stephen Foster and His Little Dog Tray
The Young Brahms